THE INTERNATIONAL WINE AND FOOD SOCIETY'S GUIDE TO

CLASSIC SAUCES
AND THEIR PREPARATION

By the same author THE FRENCH AT TABLE

THE INTERNATIONAL WINE AND FOOD SOCIETY'S GUIDE TO

CLASSIC SAUCES
AND THEIR PREPARATION

by *Raymond Oliver*

translated from the French by Rosemary Joekes

with color photographs by Kenneth Swain

and drawings by Ian Garrard

The International
Wine and Food Society

Bonanza Books
NEW YORK

A publication of
The International Wine and Food Society Limited

Bonanza Books
a division of
Crown Publishers Inc.,
419 Park Avenue South, New York 10016
© Raymond Oliver, 1967

Library of Congress Catalog Number 72-78885

This book was designed and produced by
Rainbird Reference Books Limited
Marble Arch House, 44 Edgware Road, London, w.2

Phototypeset in Monophoto Plantin by
Oliver Burridge Filmsetting Limited,
Crawley, Sussex, England
Printed and bound in Yugoslavia

House Editors: J. E. M. Hoare and Rosemary Joekes
Designer: Anthony Truscott

First published 1967
Reprinted 1972

CONTENTS

Throughout this book English measurements are given first:
the American equivalent follows in brackets

ACKNOWLEDGMENTS

The publishers and producers of this book wish to express their thanks to Paul Hamlyn Ltd, London, for permission to reproduce recipes from *Le Guide Culinaire* by Auguste Escoffier. They would like to thank Mrs Patricia Nimmo for preparing the dishes for photography.

COLOR PLATES

INTRODUCTION

For a long time I have had the impression that sauces could be counted on the fingers of one hand, and that if one were able to produce three of them, one could succeed with all the others. These three sauces are as follows:

Mayonnaise - typical of emulsified sauces

Espagnole - typical of brown sauces made with tomato

Béchamel - typical of sauces blended with flour

Like Picasso, who needed time to grow young, I too found a certain length of time was necessary to understand that a sauce is not only the fluid part of a cooked dish, but the very soul of cooking.

In my day I have taken part in some Homeric encounters. My father maintained that every food required some of its own extracts incorporated in its sauce. In practice, he did the opposite, and every day made an espagnole and a *blanquette* (a foundation sauce made with veal). He used the espagnole in any number of preparations, for example a *ris de veau* with cooked tongue, and added to the *blanquette* any excess of the sauce.

This is how *Oeufs Louis Oliver* were born. I do not know whether my father actually made *Oeufs au plat* as I have described in the recipe given below, but it is in his purest style. He always poured a thin stream of brown sauce on top of a dish of white sauce and vice versa. He was perhaps only thinking of the delicate colour scheme (a classic one in some cases), but this concession to the aesthetic sense was dear to his heart. To succeed with the authentic recipe for *Oeufs Louis Oliver*, the two sauces must be prepared beforehand.

Here is the recipe:

Warm some butter in a frying pan, or a pan suitable for cooking eggs, and gently heat a good slice of foie gras, well seasoned with salt and pepper. Cover this with a tablespoonful of chicken velouté sauce, break the eggs separately, arranging them round the pan, and cook gently. The subtle blending of the flavour of eggs, sauce and foie gras gives this dish its special aroma. When the dish is three-quarters cooked, cover the eggs with *sauce Madère* well mixed with Périgueux truffles. The cooking time must be most precisely watched, so as not to spoil the rich, smooth texture.

This recipe is the absolute negation of the principle of simplicity as it glorifies two of the three sauces Maurice Saillant detested, writing under the name of Curnonsky.

The young Saillant was very fond of my father's cooking, and he was often regaled with eggs, which otherwise he considered to be a simple hors d'oeuvre. Louis Oliver and Maurice Saillant, though their views differed on some grounds, were equally sincere; they both appreciated and loved a fine piece of work.

I will indicate the principles which signpost the long and twisting road and mark the development of sauces. These indications have been well marked and one must take a broad view of the subject.

In his *Physiology of Taste* Brillat-Savarin enunciates as his fifteenth aphorism: *On devient cuisinier, mais on nait rôtisseur* (*rôtisseurs* are born, cooks are made). In the copy which he gave to his old enemy the Marquis de Cussy, corrections in the Marquis's handwriting can be read. It seems that these corrections were made with the consent of the author before his death. One of these is concerned with this very fifteenth law, and reads: *On devient rôtisseur, mais on nait saucier* (*sauciers* (sauce chefs) are born, *rôtisseurs* are made). It seems that this definition was arrived at with some difficulty, and that the Marquis hesitated between *cuisinier* and *rôtisseur* before finally deciding. What is clear is the importance he attached to the *saucier*. There is nothing more difficult in cooking than the making of sauces. To cook asparagus, to roast veal or to sauté kidneys is certainly difficult and complicated, but it can be demonstrated, explained and learnt. But time itself is not long enough to reduce the technique of sauce making to a formula.

The *chef saucier* has, with very few exceptions, always held the position of under or second chef, when he has not been the chef himself.

Without sauces there is no true cuisine, and it can be held that the quality of a national cuisine will depend on that of its sauces. England has three hundred and sixty religions and one sauce, France one religion and three hundred and sixty sauces. Perhaps the face of the world would have been changed if, instead of mint sauce, England had possessed *sauce suprême*.

What is a sauce? I have stated earlier that it is the liquid element accompanying every culinary preparation. This is naturally not a precise definition, but it is in line with the classical academic ones. A roast served with its own liquid is not a sauce, no more than is that same liquid or gravy. Therefore a sauce is not only the liquid element although it is of the same nature and performs the same function. Nor is the fact that it is seasoned an answer, for *jus* can be salted, peppered and spiced. I would put forward this axiom: a sauce is a culinary preparation.

Although sauces are as numerous as they are varied, they can be classified into the following categories:

1. Those comprising both the essential solid and liquid elements making up the whole. Examples are *blanquette, gras double* and other *mirotons*

2. Accompanying sauces, their only solids those used as garnishing. Examples are mayonnaise, *Béarnaise* with tomato sauce, and *sauce Périgueux*

This classification is so general that it can only be vague. In practice cooks limit themselves to a very small number of different sauces, and an equally small number of procedures.

My father was without doubt a notable *saucier*. He was a 'one sauce' man, which he adapted to innumerable situations. This sauce was the espagnole and he made his *blanquette* and his velouté in exactly the same way. He prepared a *mirepoix*, (*see* Glossary, page 175). He would add hambones, bacon or ham rind and beef or veal bones. This he sprinkled with white wine, added fresh tomato purée, and cooked slowly in the oven for hours at a time. Having removed the scum and strained the stock, he would thin out the sauce. This meant boiling the liquid gently and carefully skimming the fat before storing the sauce in terrines ready for use. This was done in a meticulously careful and orderly manner.

When I say that cooking is a matter of intent, this was never more true than in the case of my father. A particularly original feature of his character was his joy in being able to use up some left-over sauce in the preparation of a meal. He thought that the preparation of a meal from some particular material would enable him to create those compositions of which he alone held the secret. When my mother justly reproached him for not being able to fix a price which would give a profitable return, he would show her the bowl with the sauce, and say 'there's our gold'. He really believed this, and it was probably true; but this kind of gold never showed a profit, for he was only truly interested in glory. He had to make money, and make it he did, but he never saved a penny.

From this I have evolved a very simple technique which can be adapted to all conditions. This is as follows: first and foremost comes the choice of vegetables. In every case use onions, carrots, celery and a bouquet garni. Depending on the final product, add garlic, shallots, roots and sprigs of parsley, turnips, green or white leeks, and fresh fennel.

Second, the fats. For brown sauces use goose fat, or that of certain roasts – pork, veal, chicken, or soft pork fat. Above all, use the fat of cured but not smoked ham or bacon, minced or chopped. For white sauces, butter mixed with oil, or chicken fat mixed with both oil and butter at the same time, is best.

Third, to moisten the sauce, use white wine or, for a brown sauce, the liquid from a roast. For white sauces, water alone can be used, while for fish sauces, either red or white wine.

Fourth, flavouring. For brown sauce a knuckle of ham, shin of veal or beef; chicken carcasses, giblets and feet of poultry, shin of veal. The bones or rind of ham previously blanched may be used for white sauces. For fish sauces, use fishbones or the heads and tails of whiting and flatfish.

METHOD

Sauté the vegetables in a large heavy saucepan or casserole. Stir with a wooden spoon. Whatever the sauce, cook the vegetables till they are soft and translucent. They should be a delicate golden colour, but should not be allowed to turn brown. Now is the time to add flour, and for the procedure known as *singeage*. This means simply adding flour and very carefully cooking it till it colours, before adding the moistening agent. The method of adding liquid is absolutely sacrosanct. Either cool the roux and add the water or other liquid hot; or add cold liquid to a hot roux. This procedure, it must be confessed, is not so important as in the case of a white sauce or velouté.

Add the bones, the shin of veal or beef, the bouquet garni, the tomato purée, if required; season and remove from the heat. Then cook in a medium oven for 3 hours. Strain first through a sieve, then a *chinois*, and lastly through a muslin cloth.

At the risk of repeating myself, let me summarize once more my father's method. He had four choices:
1. Brown sauce
2. White sauce
3. Fish sauce
4. Sauce with red wine

He followed the same method in all four cases, and varied the garnishes very little. He used pork, goose and chicken fat, or fat from roasted white meats, oil if need be, but never butter. He moistened with white wine or water. He created variety with herbs and spices, black and white pepper, nutmeg, cloves, both garlic and fennel, and made much use of celery. Tomato he used fresh, either as a purée or as concentrated extract. Beef, veal, pork and chicken were the garnishes. Depending on their size and nature, onions and other ingredients in the *mirepoix* could be put back into the sauce. This was a good idea. This type of sauce may be thick, but not too thick, as it might have to be reduced.

The gravy or extract of a roast is perfect for moistening sauce. A good stock, with the exception of fish stock, can equally well be employed for this purpose. Here perhaps some explanation is necessary. Left-overs, like a little *blanquette*, or some *sauce Périgueux* or *fond de gelée* (meat glaze), can well be used up in this way. I know that some cooks would not agree at all with my father on this point. I should like to explain the reason. Once upon a time, the *glace de viandes*, or meat glaze or concentrate, made in large kitchens, was the perquisite of the saucemaker. What was this for? And who were the buyers? It has always been a mystery to me. The usual explanation is that they were the manufacturers of concentrates, but as the amount produced would have been too small this seems improbable. To make this, an enormous stockpot must have been permanently left on the stove, where it would boil for as long as a whole year. Everything would be thrown into this, the remains of dishes, untouched helpings, the scrapings of the plates and dishes, the bones of roasts, and the feet of poultry and duck. When the *saucier* judged the stock was ready he would strain and reduce it and finally pour it into containers which would then be sold. This custom was an openly admitted and regular practice. It would happen sometimes that the *communard* (the cook responsible for cooking for the staff) would gently draw off some of the residues of the stockpot to moisten a *miroton*. This brand of theft was stigmatized by the other cooks, not because it harmed the *saucier* but because from their point of view he was putting unworthy and improper ingredients into their food. A few purists tried to bring about a reconciliation. It was, they held, impossible to make a good sauce from a heap of old rubbish. This was exactly where they were wrong, because the quality of my father's sauces left no doubt as to their excellence: that point has never been contested. The same method, however, is only permissible in the first class of sauce, known nowadays as the espagnole, or foundation brown sauce, although the definition is open to question. My father had only one rule. He never put fish in a chicken *blanquette*, although he happily put chicken *blanquette* in a fish sauce. He made a sauce with red wine exactly the same as an espagnole except that up to 80 per cent of the liquid used would be wine, and that he used little or no tomato. Again, when it came to tomatoes, I never knew whether he followed some inspiration, or whether the fact that there happened to be no tomatoes to hand decided their presence or absence in a *civet* or *sauce Chambord*. He would say with relish that his teachers had done this or that, and then deliberately do the opposite.

He did not like to make stock for a white sauce or velouté. Indeed I never saw him make an allemande. He preferred to modify a *blanquette* of veal by putting in more bones and garnishing than was necessary, and by using more liquid. Ample as this was, it could then be used for two purposes: as a *blanquette*, certainly, but in addition as a velouté with more than one use. My father never used the familiar method of browning the flour in a *blanquette*. Since the results were admirable, one must suppose that he was gifted. My father believed that every food bears within it the requisite elements for the making of its own sauce, and also the method of supplementing a preparation with a foundation sauce. His method of cooking calves' or beef tongues, sweetbreads, calves' feet or pigs' trotters, all in a foundation sauce, demonstrated this theory. He never had a special method of cooking these dishes. He would put them aside or finish them as his fancy took him. I sometimes wondered if these methods were not a form of excuse for laziness.

He was no lover of béchamel sauce but there were occasions when he simply had to make it or arrange for it to be made. He preferred an alternative solution to the classical method. He would exercise his judgement in this. The milk was boiled with thyme or bay leaves and seasoned with nutmeg, salt and cayenne pepper, before being blended with the roux. Or another time finely chopped onions would be reduced over the fire and boiled with the sauce till it was creamy.

I think we have discussed my father long enough, and it is time to turn our attention to sauces and the important part they have played in the evolution of cooking.

Can sauces be classified? The attempt must be made. There are the great classical brown and white foundation sauces: espagnole and béchamel, velouté and allemande; tomato sauces; wine sauces; emulsified sauces (hot and cold sauces made with oil and vinegar) and those which include some solids, however they are prepared. There are, moreover, some sauces which fit into none of these categories.

The work of the *sauciers* of the past must not be ignored, but it will perhaps be more difficult to prophesy what the future will hold for the art of the *saucier*. Therefore we will review the sauces of the recent and remote past in order to arrive at modern methods which will determine the future of our cuisine. From the whispers of the early days of gastronomy in the era of Christianity, we know that sauces were an essential part of cookery. It must be admitted that cooks never thought to describe their methods of roasting which they considered either common knowledge or too uninteresting to be worth describing. Sauces were presented as dishes and not merely as condiments. In a good stew, onions were mixed with spices, song-thrushes, honey and almonds. Sauces were always made with honey or sugar, vinegar or wine, spices, almonds and herbs. Onions, garlic and shallots appeared in nearly every preparation, but it would seem that the *fond*, or foundation sauce as we know it, did not appear until the Renaissance. A single accompanying sauce was used, or abused, either with oysters, vegetables or fish. It would be sprinkled on a dish of sow's udders *à la sauce Lucullus*, or used as a *purée à l'Héliogabale*. This sauce was *garum*. Either because, once again, the method of preparation was considered very easy, or because it was not, strictly speaking, a recipe at all, we have not inherited the means of making *garum*. We have only our imaginations, which are probably not far from the truth.

Garum in its simplest form is an extract of the juices from fish of the mackerel family, young tunny fish and other similar fish. There is a Vietnamese condiment called *Nuoc-mam* which must be very nearly the same. To this the Romans would add honey, vinegar, water, the livers of mullet and *murennae* (lampreys), sea urchin coral and anchovy purée.

To those of us who like Far Eastern cookery, this would not be out of the ordinary. However, to Western tastes it is an unusual mixture.

The Romans looked for symbols and respected them. A Roman would eat *animellae* to shine before his mistress, which made nobody laugh but fools, and if an intellectual or philosopher smiled it would only be from jealousy.

In themselves, sauces were not symbolic. Their function was as an accompaniment, and to serve as a disguise. In making the 'food of love', a sauce could be either a phyltre or be employed simply to hide an aphrodisiac. It is clear that there must have been many other sauces before the appearance of *garum*, but none has been so intriguing or given rise to so much research among real gourmets, that studious, ill-defined race. Perhaps this is the moment to cast an eye over possible definitions. What in effect is a gourmet? Some people make a profession out of it, and are by popular definition 'parasites'. Such people are a purely imaginary race. Ask your friends. They will not be able to give a single example. There are some who are gourmets by vocation. They write, in greater or lesser quantity, about matters of the table. There are good ones and bad ones among them, just as there are good and bad cooks, restaurateurs or bistros.

Finally there are the true dilettantes, who have a genuine and disinterested passion for the subject. These are the people who, swathing themselves in an apron, approach the cooking stove in the spirit of Ali-Baba to attempt some transcendental preparation. They will sometimes make a good dish, but always modestly. They are quickly convinced that amateurism is a sin. They persevere for the joy of testing, trying, blunting their talents on invisible difficulties. They will try out a dish a hundred times to perfect it. These are they who will go to a restaurant, order the meal objectively, are sparing with their compliments and know how to show displeasure. These are the people, who because they have educated tastes, can tell the difference between one truffle and another. For truffles alone are not enough to make a dish good. Bitter *foie gras* has been known and also greasy, salty caviars. Could one say the true gourmet is not just a man who lives entirely upon ortolans and thinks there is no virtue in having pheasant except with lentils, but a man who accords each dish its due merits? One should not believe that the gourmet is a rare and disappearing specimen. Not at all; he is, however, modest and he must be sought out. He knows that cooking is an art and that one must love it to appreciate it. He is frightened of missing something, and if somebody tells him that the best *pocheuse* is *chez* Culinace he will go and try it. Unconvinced, he will pay with a good grace, please everybody with a smile whose secret irony he alone knows, and make a mental note never to come back again. If a man tells you that he is a gourmet, be as wary of him as if he had told you that he is a man of intelligence. Some decent modesty is necessary. The sauce is the testing ground of a gourmet. It is as difficult as the squaring of the circle. The gourmet appreciates at their true worth,

the fine points of an exceptional butter, a ripe cheese, or bread baked in a
wood-fired oven. The success of a sauce will depend for him upon both its
quality as a dish and the setting of the meal. Do you know the story of the
smoker who one day bought the pipe of his dreams? He came home,
settled himself by the fire, carefully filled the bowl with the best mixture,
lit up and drew on it with pleasure. Then he wished to put his pipe on the
ashtray beside his armchair. He was horrified at its mean vulgarity and
hurried off to buy another one. Placing this in his 'smoking room' he
understood that he had lived far too long in unworthy and shabby sur-
roundings . . . and so, in the end, he changed his house – all because he had
bought a pipe! The gourmet will find himself in the same position. If you
place truffles before him without notifying of what is in store for him,
he will be faced with a multiplication of difficulties; having to find agree-
able companions, wines or accessories.

For many of us sauces evoke tomato, onion, herbs, cream, yolks of eggs
and butter. It is to be understood that tomato sauces are post-Columbus,
that cream and butter only became popular with the Renaissance, but that
there had been sauces in some form before this. We have often asked ourselves if trying to eat sauce with the fingers did not present insoluble
problems, but anyone who has ever seen Arabs eating *couscous* with their
fingers without dirtying their robes will appreciate that it is possible. Not
everybody ate like Henry VIII. To make things easier, at the last minute
they added toasted breadcrumbs to the sauce previously prepared by the
galopin (the scullion responsible for toasting bread and running errands).
The idea was to absorb the sauce and make it more manageable.

Our ideas on this subject are quite different from those adopted by our
ancestors. To them the sauce was a means of cooking much more than an
accompaniment. Study of the etymological definition of the word sauce
shows that, in the Middle Ages there was confusion between sauces and
marinades. The word *sauce* was gascon in origin, evolved from *sauco*, in
itself a derivation of the Latin word saltus, meaning salted. The train of
thought is clear. Meat preserved in salt will exude a salty liquid, the '*sauce*'.
To salt meat became, in effect, to put meat in a sauce. A marinade in the
modern sense is not far removed from this concept. A marinade must not
be confused with a sauce. Rare indeed, however, were the marinades which
were not used in the production of the sauces. One could however, without
doing the wrong thing ignore the liquid, as we too often do today in the

case of the liquid in which prawns are cooked: very few gourmets know how good that is to taste.

Naturally enough, the intention of the first chefs was to produce a sauce so rich that the little that could be absorbed was sufficient.

At this point one must mention the important part played by vinegars in the kitchen before Escoffier's time. In the Middle Ages wine, as we know it, was practically unknown. It existed only in exceptionally good years. There was often very little difference between certain poor wines and the vinegar made from them. Good quality vinegar depends more on the purity than on the quality of the wine. The first of all antacids was honey, and later sugar. The first sauce makers were caramelists. Caramel was of course really sugar cane. Spices and sugar were therefore indispensable in the creation of sauces. When we think we have invented something new by poaching slices of pineapple in syrup before adding them to duck or roast foods, we are only repeating the actions of a thousand years ago. The result of a reduction of caramel in vinegar with the later addition of juices and preserves is a perfect example of reversion to the sauces of the Middle Ages.

The contemporaries of Charles Martel ate in exactly the same manner as their enemies the Moors, and the subjects of Charles V were scarcely more refined than the soldiers of Tamburlaine.

To sum up, our forebears used to boil meat, vegetables, fish and spices, strain them from the pan, and so lived by taking pot-luck.

COOKERY TERMS, PROCESSES AND TECHNIQUES

Explanation is necessary of some of the French cookery terms and processes to be found in the discussion of basic principles and in the recipes of this book. These recipes have been drawn from many sources, which illustrate the development of sauces throughout the course of centuries.

I only use technical terms once they have been explained, and then only when there is no alternative. Technical language, which becomes incomprehensible to the outsider, is often the shortest and clearest method of communicating information between professional or other workers in the same field. Explanations of such terms are often confusing, and I have therefore tried to be clear and simple. To avoid too many cross-references to precise definitions, I may sometimes repeat myself in the text with an explanation.

BAIN-MARIE

This term describes a method of cooking by indirect heat using a kind of double saucepan or container. The cooking pot, bowl or pan is set in another larger one containing water. The water will be boiling, hot, or merely warm, depending on whether the food is to be cooked or merely kept warm. So a *bain-marie* serves a double purpose, either to cook a sauce or to keep it hot.

Whether the *bain-marie* is to be used for cooking or conservation must depend on the context of your recipe. Béchamel, velouté, *Mornay* and *demi-glace* sauces can all be kept hot by this method. It is not recommended for hot emulsified sauces, contrary to the usual advice, for they are too fragile and are apt to disintegrate. It is better to stand this kind of sauce in a warm place, not too close to a fierce heat.

Many other kinds of dish may be kept hot in this way, so much so that many manufacturers of kitchen utensils have abandoned later methods and returned to it. A particular type of specialized saucepan called a *bain-marie* is now on sale. Enamelled inside and out, it is rather tall and narrow, with a short handle at the top of the pan. This facilitates standing it in the outer pan or bath. The difference between a true *bain-marie* and a double saucepan or steamer is that the water surrounds the inner pan and is not merely in contact with the bottom of it.

BEURRER

To butter. This word is used in two senses in cookery. It can mean simply adding a certain quantity of butter to a sauce, as in *sauce bâtarde*. More often it is applied to spreading butter on the surface of a sauce to avoid the formation of a skin. Little pats of butter are dotted all over the surface. This must be done when the sauce is still hot and before the skin is formed. Another method is to cut a round of paper slightly bigger than the top of the container, grease it with butter and place it on the surface of the sauce, buttery side down. Greasing the paper may not be necessary if air is completely excluded from the sauce and the paper is damp enough to stick to the surface. If the sauce is going to be reheated the amount of butter is not important.

BLANCHIR

To blanch. This term is applied to sauce making in two ways; only one is relevant, and that rather indirectly. Firstly, it concerns the preparation of a sauce in which vegetables, potatoes, celery hearts, or veal for a *blanquette* are covered with cold water in a deep receptacle and brought to boiling point, boiled for a moment and then taken out and plunged into cold water. Some foods are blanched to get rid of acidity or to keep them fresh. In Gascony, blanching has another meaning. There it means to add eggs and vinegar to a sauce. This method is good for fish sauces and *blanquettes*. This can be confused with blending, which it apparently resembles. But here it means to whiten in the literal sense of the word. A creamy sauce will turn white with a little milk and a drop of vinegar. This is an old-fashioned method, and today it is done with cream and lemon juice.

CASSER

To break. In culinary terms, a sauce 'breaks' when an emulsion disintegrates; the different elements then separate and the sauce curdles. This is a minor problem when it happens in the kitchen. But if it happens on the way to the table it may be troublesome. It is often caused by a too hot dish or by the sauce remaining too long on a hot plate. A spoonful of hollandaise will put this right.

CLARIFIER

There are many methods of clarification, but they are rarely relevant to sauces. Let us agree that they are chemical changes which turn an opaque liquid into a clear one. The best known method is that of using lightly whisked white of egg. As this congeals it attracts the solid matter suspended in the liquid. All that remains to be done is to filter the liquid and then decant it to obtain a crystal clear liquid.

Clarified butter is first melted and then its scum removed, i.e. the milky froth. It will now be a clear yellow liquid with the character and appearance of oil, according to the temperature at which it has been clarified. I am aware that some chefs prefer not to clarify the butter used in making emulsified sauces. This is justified by the acid quality and the taste given by this milk. This emphasizes that there are no hard and fast rules in cookery.

To clarify a sauce and turn it into a jelly as in the case of the recipe for Guinea Fowl Château Guiraud (*see* page 112) this method is used.

Chop parsley, tarragon and celery leaves very finely; there should be about 3½ oz. in all. Add the white of an egg and beat lightly, but keeping the white of egg liquid.

Add the gravy from the guinea fowl, which must be tepid – whisk together, pour into a thick bottomed saucepan and cook over a low fire, stirring until the temperature is just below boiling point. Don't boil. Leave at the side of the cooker for 10–15 minutes. Strain.

Some cooks add an eggshell at the same time as the white. It is a technique which should help in clarifying; it is certainly a good way of using up egg shells!

DÉCANTER

To decant. In sauce making this means the removal of ingredients used to make the sauce but unwanted in the final result. Used only with reference to composite sauce dishes such as ragoûts, *civets*, *capilotades*. These may include a *mirepoix*, with unskinned garlic, large onions, green leeks and so on. For large quantities use a cloth, for small ones a strainer. Pour the sauce over the cloth stretched over a bowl. Pick out from the cloth the meat and vegetables wanted for the final dish; dip them in the sauce and place in a clean dish. Strain the sauce a second time through a conical sieve over the pieces of meat, garnish afresh if necessary with baby glazed onions, mushrooms and so on. The sauce can be blended between these two operations.

For small quantities lift the pieces out with a skimmer and place them in the fresh dish, then proceed as above.

This procedure is much in use at the present day and is obligatory in many cases. Taking the treatment of *blanquette* as a classical example, there are three possible methods of 'decanting':

1. The direct method, in which the vegetables are cut up neatly beforehand. The meat may or may not be returned to the sauce after decanting; both methods are acceptable. Add flour, liquid, bouquet garni, stir and cook. Remove the bouquet, blend, and the dish is ready.
2. Indirect method. Exactly the same as above, but the sauce is cooked before it is decanted. Then strain it, blend and pour it over the meat. Garnishing may be added with discretion.
3. In this method the meat and vegetables are prepared as before. The bouquet garni, garnishes and seasoning are added. When the meat is cooked, decant the sauce. This procedure should be done after making the roux, for the sauce is otherwise perfectly clear.

Sometimes butter muslin can be used to avoid the messy side of decanting. This procedure may be necessary after such a small mishap as the breaking of the string round a bouquet garni.

DÉGLACER

To deglaze. This is one of those terms for which a whole descriptive passage is necessary in English. It means to scrape the bottom of a roasting tin, stewpan or saucepan to release the concentrated reduction of sauce, cooking fluid or juices left after cooking. If any fat has been used, this must first be removed, leaving the light or dark brown skin or jelly. Release this from the bottom and blend with water, or in some cases, wine or cream.

In discussing *déglaçage*, it is necessary to mention *glace*, which in referring to a sauce always means a concentrated reduction. The term *tomber à glace* or *faire tomber à glace* means to reduce as much as possible. I have spoken elsewhere (*see* page 37) about *glace de viande* or meat glaze. However, in many recipes it is necessary to reduce the sauce to a glaze every time.

As reduction is a deliberate act, it would seem absurd to deglaze, since that would mean that the volume of the preparation would be brought up to its original level. But in fact this is not necessarily the same thing, as the liquid, which may be wine, water or fresh stock, when added to the glaze should add nobility and flavour.

DÉGRAISSER

In sauce making this means removing fat from the surface of the sauces. Aromas are preserved and held captive in fat, which is mistaken for a fixative. In fact, it holds and contains flavour. For this reason, fatty sauces are often very attractive. Specialists often use rich fats, taken from sauces, to fry *pommes fondantes*.

DÉPOUILLER

To skim. Literally to skin. It means to remove fat or scum from a sauce or stock. When you have done this and taken off the fat, the sauce is skimmed. This is not quite true. In doing this, the sauce maker is aiming at an impossible perfection. A really good sauce maker who intends to do this thoroughly will repeat the process several times, straining the sauce through a tammy cloth or a strainer, boiling it again, removing the fat and scum, and will strain and restrain through finer and finer sieves or muslins removing impurities (or what are taken to be impurities). In modern cookery sauces are lighter and less complicated. They are still skimmed but this is achieved much more simply than in previous centuries.

DÉSSÉCHER

Drying out is seldom used in the making of sauces. Dry-roasting meat is comparable.

DÉTENDRE

To condense a sauce is very difficult, to lengthen it very easy. Those most often lengthened are béchamel and *Mornay*. Lengthening a sauce means thinning, making the sauce more liquid. Only sauces are lengthened and these two above all. The liquid used depends on the type of sauce. Lengthen *Mornay*, béchamel and velouté sauces with milk and cream. Consommé may also be used, either broth or clear stock. Brown sauces may be lengthened with Madeira, white wine, clear stock or soup.

It is best to do this when the sauce is ready for use. Remember there is always a risk of curdling.

ÉCUMER

To skim. This procedure, although little used in the final stages, can be a very important one in the initial preparation. It means simply to remove the scum which rises to the surface, whatever its nature.

ÉTUVER

Strictly speaking, this refers to *cuisson à l'étuvé*, cooking in a tightly closed utensil without moistening. This is not done where sauces are concerned. The method is not applied to a sauce but to the different ingredients in the composition. It means to stew something in its own juice. This can be done with vegetables and certain meats cooked at the same time as the vegetables. *Petits pois à l'étuvé* are a classical example; tiny onions, celery hearts, fennel, artichoke, leeks also.

The commonest method is quickly to colour the vegetables in butter, cover the pan and leave to cook over a low heat. Therefore sauce garnishes are cooked by this means. Considering that mushrooms may be so prepared, the importance of this method can be seen.

FAIRE FONDRE

This means literally to melt, to dissolve. In sauce making, this term is applied to vegetables and above all to onions, garlic and leeks. It is really a figure of speech, because they do not actually dissolve, but become translucent and soft. They are used as a base. The onions may be chopped or cut into thin slices. Start cooking them over a moderate flame and then continue very gently without a lid and at the side of the fire or heat. (*Tomber* and *faire fondre* mean much the same thing.)

FAIRE REVENIR

It is one of the most up-to-date cookery terms. It means to colour, to brown slightly. *Revenir* implies a wooden spoon and the shaking of the saucepan.

This process is used especially with vegetables and meats used in the composition of a sauce. These processes are sometimes more complex than they appear at first sight.

The process can be described quite simply thus: after cooking the meat for a few minutes over a brisk fire, remove it, drain it. Add the vegetables to the cooking fat and as soon as they have browned slightly or changed colour, put back the meat, drained as shown above and kept in reserve. Pounded tomatoes, a bouquet garni and water will be added before seasoning and cooking.

FILTRER

To strain and to sieve. Means to filter in the strict sense of the word. Nowadays stock for sauces is scarcely ever filtered. Stock and sauces should first be poured through a strainer or a sieve, then through a *chinois* and finally a tammy or a butter muslin cloth. A *chinois* is a conical metal strainer, shaped like a Chinese coolie hat.

Some sauces should be strained through a tammy cloth, others are better through muslin. The operation is carried out in two stages. The sauce is put in the cloth and the ends folded over. Two people are needed to hold the cloth, which is then pulled gently from each end and the sauce rubbed through by holding two wooden spoons in one hand. This excellent method, used for brown and game sauces and other varieties of espagnole, is gradually being given up.

Other sauces, above all emulsified sauces like *Béarnaise*, should be strained through muslin but in a different way. Drape the muslin over an enamelled bowl or pan. Pour the sauce into the muslin, taking care that the edges of the cloth do not slip into the dish, which would let the sauces soak up over the edges. Two pairs of hands are again needed to lift and wring the cloth in opposite directions. The liquid sauce will be squeezed through. Scrape the outside with a wooden spoon.

There are many pieces of equipment, more or less suitable, which today make these procedures much easier and eliminate laborious methods. There are *moulis* and blenders, hair sieves and mills.

Some sauces must always be strained, while others such as *blanquettes* and ragoûts will be perfectly satisfactory without this. They are, I believe, better decanted (*q.v.*).

FRISSONNER

To bubble or roll. Sauces hardly ever bubble, but some of the foundations such as *fumets* are allowed to be treated thus. Liquid sings as it bubbles. Without being too precise about the exact temperature, it can be said that all liquids *frissonnent* when the surface begins to move and roll, but before it boils. If this liquid is water-based this will happen at just under 212°F. (100°C.). The boiling points of liquids vary considerably, those of fats being always higher than water, and that of sugar even higher. Some fats have a lower melting and boiling point than others, pork being lower than beef for example.

INCORPORER

To incorporate. When a garnish, butter, cream or liquid is absorbed by a sauce, it is said to be incorporated. There is, with reason, some confusion with *monter* (*see* page 30), but to the professional, incorporating refers to the adding of some out-of-the-ordinary ingredient to a sauce. One would quite naturally say 'add some purée of foie gras' whereas, more properly, in this case, one should say 'incorporate'. Incorporating also carries the implication that it is performed during the final stages of a preparation.

LIER

To blend. The subject of blending is one of the first importance. It would be possible to start all over again and write a complete book on the subject. Moreover, as we shall see, blending and thickening may be one and the same thing. By definition, to blend is to thicken, but it also implies giving a rich smooth texture. To blend means to balance and unite different constituents as well as to bind them together. Often, this means emulsification. Blending may be achieved by the following combinations of ingredients:

1. Fats, with or without the addition of yolks of eggs. This combination is used above all in soups, such as *potage Germiny*, and veloutés. A typical example is 1 tablespoonful of cream to the yolk of 1 egg added to the sauce; but beware of bringing the sauce to boiling point, the enemy of success. It may certainly be brought *up to* boiling point, but this is risky and skill and timing are needed. This is why one is usually advised to avoid the attempt. It is permissible to use a *bain-marie* to avoid the risk of ruining the sauce.

2. Fats with flour or starches (cornflour, etc). Sauces such as *Bordelaise* or *Bercy* are blended with this combination. *Beurre-manié* is the standard example. Mix softened butter with flour and add to a runny sauce. To obtain a good liaison take care to keep whisking throughout the operation and do not add too much of the *beurre-manié* at a time. *Beurre-manié* is in some ways an uncooked roux. It is very easy to prepare, as the softened butter absorbs the flour without the risk of lumps forming. Certain ragoûts as well as sauces are blended with *beurre-manié*; also *petits pois* and other vegetable preparations which may be used in garnished sauces.

3. Flour, cornflours and meals with liquid – port, sherry, white wine, liqueurs, spirits, water.

The most characteristic example of this type of blend is potato flour mixed with Madeira added to meat juices or gravy to thicken them. This is the method used in the preparation of *sauce Madère, sauce Périgueux* or a *demi-glace*. It can equally be applied to thick soups.

MIJOTER

Simmering can be ruinous or have a touch of genius. It is synonymous both with good cooking and bad. If one does not wish to use an iconoclastic term, let it be said that *mijoter* is typical of middle class cookery.

Mijoter means to cook gently for a long time. It means to many, besides, to reheat in similar conditions. To simmer means to take one's time, to take longer than normal. It is to wait for some imaginary perfection, thanks to some subtle alchemy. I have a theory that when a dish tastes better reheated, it has not been properly cooked in the first place. There are of course exceptions.

MONTER

To rise. In culinary terms, this is the technique (meaning literally to rise, to mount up, to make up) of adding a liquid little by little to hot and cold emulsified sauces. The liquid may be oil or melted butter. But in some cases, e.g. fish or some brown sauces, or *sauce bâtarde*, softened butter may be added at the last moment. This is much the same process as moistening a sauce with a roux incorporated in it, or when using the technique of *vannage*. But this process must be done with infinitely more care and attention than is necessary for moistening. It is not necessary to exaggerate the precautions required, but the cook, while being careful, need not be timid.

NAPPER

To coat. In the explanation of *vanner* (*see* page 32) this has been discussed at length. However, there are two aspects of this word to consider: the coating action itself and, secondly, its bearing on the consistency of the sauce. As the sauce will ultimately be used to coat food which may be hot or cold, it must be able to do this properly. Moreover, we are concerned with the consistency of the sauce and, above all, the ease with which it serves its purpose. To coat something properly the sauce must be neither too fluid nor too thick. It must cling, mould and not disguise the food it covers. Almost anything may be coated with sauce, with more or less happy results.

RÉDUIRE

To reduce. Reducing is the touchstone of the sauce maker's skill. My father used to say that a badly reduced sauce tasted like wax. It is a perfect simile, although I do not think my father actually ate wax himself! It is quite clear that the best results are obtained from the interaction of reducing and building up, or strengthening. I think that reduction is imcompatible with simmering. It should be said that reducing is the mark of a great chef, a sauce maker; simmering is typical of honest housewives. Earlier it has been said that simmering is feminine, reducing masculine. I discuss reducing elsewhere (*see* pages 64, 81).

RESSERRER

To tighten. This process means literally to tighten up or pull a sauce together. In practice this means thickening, but it is not the same thing as blending. Blending a sauce may thicken it, but not necessarily pull it together. But tightening up a sauce means, to the professional, something quite different. It is easier to do this at an earlier than at a later stage of preparation. The classic way to *resserrer* is to go back to the beginning by making up some fresh roux and adding it to the sauce. This is really intended to rectify a mistake. It is much easier to make the preparation sufficiently thick to allow for lengthening it if need be; lengthening being the opposite of tightening. The sauces most commonly treated in this way are *Mornay*, béchamel and velouté.

RISSOLER

To fry. Rissoles in French cookery are little pastries (mostly puff) stuffed with forcemeat and then fried in deep fat. *Rissoler* has come to mean to fry very lightly, to colour, to sauté. Butter (or a mixture of butter and oil) is melted in a heavy frying pan or a *sauteuse*, and then chopped vegetables, sliced onions, or small pieces of meat or chicken are very gently cooked over a low flame until they change colour, brown, or become translucent as required. Stir with a wooden spoon during the cooking or keep turning over lightly with a two-pronged fork.

SINGER

To sprinkle, to dust. The origin of the term (which means literally to ape or mimic) is not known. It means, in culinary parlance, to dust or sprinkle meat or vegetables lightly with flour during cooking, and then to cook them lightly. This term is also applied to preparing a roux, although here it does not refer to sprinkling. In this context the flour is put all at once into the pan, mixed with butter or some other fat and then cooked. In this sense it is the second stage of preparing a roux. I believe it to be essential in sauce making. There is a school of thought which despises the use of flour, corn-flour or ground rice, maize or meals. Yet all sauce makers make use of these ingredients as well as arrowroot.

One way of using this method involves anticipating the results. It is difficult to explain, but in brief it can be said that a sauce which has been lightly sprinkled with flour will reduce and blend better than one which has not been so treated.

It is not always necessary to sprinkle a sauce with flour as described, since certain sauces, although they should be reduced, ought to remain runny. A light touch is called for. Most young chefs err in the opposite direction, and so this kind of work is rarely entrusted to them. My father would always be happy to let an unskilled assistant prepare a *mirepoix* or a *brunoise* (*see* Glossary) before the liquid is added; but he would insist on adding and cooking the flour himself. In this he was following tradition. The day the junior was permitted to *singer* a sauce or a roux was equivalent to the long awaited occasion when the flying instructor hands over the stick to the pupil to make his first solo flight.

The importance of this technique in the making of sauces ought not to be minimized.

STABILISER

To stabilize a sauce is much the same as binding or gluing it together. The technique is little used today. It is done to prevent the breakdown of an emulsion by using ground rice, arrowroot and certain cornflours and cereal meals. In practice it may be ignored.

VANNER

Skin formation and its prevention. *Vanner* means literally to winnow or to fan, but it is a word not now in use. In cookery terms it describes the method of preventing a skin forming on the surface of a sauce. Thirty-five years ago when I used to discuss with my father the proper basis for one method or another, this one appeared to us already out of date. Still, the modern methods of buttering surfaces with or without using paper are not enough.

If you want the sauce to be absolutely smooth and without any lumps whatsoever, the classical procedure must be carried out. The idea is to cool the sauce without any lumps or skin forming. This is achieved by keeping the sauce in motion while it is cooling. Stir continually with a wooden spatula. Keep moving it away from the sides of the pan or receptacle. This is most important, for if care is not taken, the sauce will cool from the outside inwards, leading to lumps.

Some sauces are intended to be used cold, although they were made hot in the first place. *Chaud-froid* is a good example of this type. A *chaud-froid* is nothing more or less than a gelatinous velouté used cold. It may be used to cover a dish or to coat it. If the sauce is not meant to be a coat, skinning is useful but not absolutely necessary; but if the sauce is intended for a coating it is essential. There are two ways to 'jellify' a sauce. Either use calves' foot jelly, chicken legs and beef or veal shinbones, or simply add gelatine.

THE CLASSIFICATION
OF SAUCES,
STOCKS AND GLAZES

In the past, *fonds blancs*, glazes, roux, *gelées*, stocks, *nages* and marinades were all classified as sauces.

It seems logical that a glaze could be considered a sauce, but I will not enlarge on this. My subject is sauces and present day ideas about them, and to dwell on the subject would be doubly useless as it would in the first place be tedious, and in the second lead to confusion, whereas I wish to make clarity my aim.

Elsewhere I speak of *fond blanc*, which is clear stock. Once upon a time everything was moistened with *fond blanc*. This was overdone, and indeed, whenever liquid was added to a preparation this meant stock and not water. *Fond blanc* was a colourless clear soup made by boiling together beef bones and vegetables. This broth was skimmed, seasoned with herbs and cloves and then left to simmer until cooked. It was then strained and was ready for use. It was understood that the better the quality of these foundation stocks and the more care taken over their proportions and preparations, the better the result would be.

COURT-BOUILLON

The dividing line between *court-bouillon* and *nage* is not clear, just as in the case of veal stock and a *demi-glace*. It means an aromatic preparation for use in boiling a joint, galantine, fish or shell-fish. In my opinion, it is not a sauce. However, it may be included in the composition of certain sauces in the same way as is clear soup or foundation white stock.

FONDS

Fonds are the foundations upon which sauces are built. Curnonsky said he hated them for, if mediocre, they would ruin the quality of the sauce by bringing everything down to their own level. They still have a place, though of less importance, in fine cooking, even though of a simple order.

FUMETS

What is the difference between *fonds* and *fumets*? Virtually none. In fact, the term *fumet* is used for certain *fonds* without the reason being known. The same is true for the word *coulis* or purée, i.e., *coulis* of shrimps, lobster, tomato or game. To some extent, the same confusion exists with the use of the word *bisque*. One thing is certain; without fear of error one can describe a *coulis concentré*, a *fumet* or a *bisque* equally well by the word *fond*, or foundation. If I ask my chef: 'Have you any shell-fish stock?' he will answer that, yes, he has *Américaine*, i.e. lobster stock, or a concentrate or a *bisque*. The word *fond* tends to be used for everything and, because of this, the term is sometimes despised.

The number of different foundation stocks may be reduced and, in practice, there is only one which is essential for the cook – *fond de veau*, or veal stock. This is used in conjunction with clear or blended stock. All the others may be prepared if necessary, and in conjunction with the menu.

It is likely that one would prepare a white stock prior to developing this into consommé. The two processes are interwoven. My father, however, made the soup straight away without going through the intermediate phase of a white stock. This method is more difficult and impractical in a restaurant kitchen. The same holds good for fish and lobster *fumet*, *bisque* and so on. However, if a fish sauce were on the menu, it would be necessary to prepare in advance a fish stock for cooking sole, turbot, brill etc. This is what is done nowadays. In the past it was a little different. In the old days they not only prepared veal stock (thick or clear), but also espagnole, allemande, chicken and fish veloutés, composite and emulsified sauces.

Nowadays in the Grand Véfour we prepare, daily, veal stock, *Béarnaise*, hollandaise, *Mornay* and *Américaine* sauces besides, of course, the sauces necessary for the menu of that day, e.g. *Soubise*, *Villeroy*, *Choron*, *mousquetaire*, *Mireille*, etc.

It must be admitted that *fond* is a portmanteau word with a chameleon-like quality, but it is one which can be widely applied. We will not need to define it in greater detail except for *fond clair* and *fond lié*, clear and thick stock.

GLACE

A *glace* was the result of the maximum reduction of a basic sauce. Pride of place went to meat *glace*; then followed fish, chicken and game. A meat *glace* is obtained by slowly reducing unsalted veal stock. Some precautions must be taken. The stock must be strained through a tammy cloth whenever the casserole in which it is being cooked is changed and the pan must be stirred constantly. The final result will look like soft toffee. It is used to enhance insipid flavours.

FOND (OR JUS) DE VEAU LIÉ (thick veal stock)

After preparing a clear veal stock, as described below, strain it through a muslin cloth and blend with cornflour stirred into a little Maderia, to prevent lumps. This is used in much the same way as clear *fond de veau*.

FOND DE VEAU

The method employed follows very closely the one used by chefs at the beginning of this century.

Veal bones are broken and then placed in a roasting tin. A thick *mirepoix* of vegetables consisting of chopped onions, carrots and turnips is added. These are browned in the oven, taking care not to burn the ingredients. This precaution is very necessary because overbrowning is the sauce-maker's great mistake. If you wish to have a dark colour, it is better to roast an onion with its skin still on. There is a big difference in taste between charred bones and a roasted onion. The contents of the roasting tin are then turned out into a stockpot and sufficient water added and a pinch of salt to every 2 lb. of bones. Then add good nourishing ingredients, without going to the lengths of previous generations which were capable of adding a whole shoulder of fat meat. Shin bones with poultry or veal gravy are quite good enough.

Let the stock come to the boil and skim. Add fresh vegetables, leeks, celery and a bouquet garni. Bring to the boil again, skim once more and then simmer uncovered for six hours. Strain through a metal strainer, bring to the boil again and pour through a conical strainer or a linen cloth, boil up for the last time and put aside until required for use.

This is in fact an ideal use for parings and for over-ripe tomatoes; in practice one does add a little tomato though theoretically none is required. Today, tomatoes are available the whole year round, and we use them all the time.

This sort of basic stock preparation is really meant for large scale or commercial use, and is only of interest to the professional cook. For example, take a housewife who wants to make a veal stock to use, perhaps for a pepper steak. Of course, she can make it by reducing the quantities and using a saucepan, or casserole, instead of a large stock-pot. She will need about 5 pints (6¼ pints) of water to a little over 2 lb. of bones, and the vegetables and seasoning as shown above. This will give a minimum of about 1⅔ pints (2¼ pints) of sauce, which is still a lot. If care is taken not to season more than the proportion of a pinch of salt to 2 lb. of bones, it is possible to reduce the quantity far more. But reducing is not an easy task for the housewife, so she should use a different method.

GELÉE
This may be confused with consommé or clarified stock. Generally speaking, it is more full-bodied than consommé and tastier. It can be a natural jelly, made from calves' feet, shin bones and so on, or an artificial one made by adding gelatine.

MARINADE
A *marinade* is a seasoned liquid in which foodstuffs are steeped. Oil, wine, vinegar, herbs and spices may be included. In considering vinegar and its place in cooking, *marinades* hold an important place. In the same way as *fonds* they may be included in the preparation of a sauce as part of the 'moistening' process. Some cooked *marinades* are very close to being sauces, since they contain all the ingredients. In my opinion, however, they must not be so classified because they are becoming rarer in practice, and this would present a problem to the younger generation. In the past *marinades* played an important part in preservation, an asset which the general use of refrigeration has made unnecessary.

ROUX

Roux is a blend of flour and fat. Today butter and flour are commonly used for this purpose. The longer the mixture is cooked, the deeper will be the colour obtained. Roux can be white and hardly cooked at all, pale yellow when it is cooked for a short time, or brown when well cooked. The pale yellow or biscuit-coloured roux is the one most used.

SIMPLIFIED BASIC STOCK

1 lb. bones
1 onion
1⅔ pints (2¼ pints) water
1 tomato
bouquet garni
large glass of white wine
1 carrot
celery
2 cloves
bunch of fresh herbs (or dried herbs)

Break 1 lb. best marrow bones. Place in an ovenproof casserole to brown in the oven with the onion cut in two. Add the water and other ingredients, bring to the boil, skim and simmer for a good 2 hours, in the oven. Strain.

PEPPER STEAK (*Steak au Poivre*)
Illustrating the use of a clear veal stock.

about ½ lb. steak per serving
1 teaspoonful crushed black peppercorns
salt
1 tablespoonful oil
1 tablespoonful butter
4 tablespoonfuls veal stock
2 tablespoonfuls Cognac
2 oz. (¼ cup) butter

In a shallow pan or casserole heat the butter and oil briskly. Salt the steak all over and force the crushed pepper into the surface by pressing hard (this operation to be done at the last possible minute). Sear the steaks in the pan and turn them over as quickly as possible. Continue cooking them over a moderate heat. When they are done to your taste, drain the fat from the pan, add the Cognac and set it alight.

Withdraw the steaks and place them on a serving dish. Pour the veal stock into the same pan, place it over a fierce heat and reduce by two-thirds. Take the pan from the fire and add the butter, little by little, stirring all the time. Pour the sauce over the steaks and serve with soufflé potatoes.

TRUFFLE OMELETTE (*Omelette aux Truffes*)
Illustrating the use of a thick veal stock.
6 servings:

5 eggs
salt (no pepper)
3 oz. fresh raw truffles
6 tablespoonfuls thick veal stock
I tablespoonful Cognac
butter
oil

Beat the eggs after adding salt sparingly. Chop up the truffles and fry them gently in butter. Add the Cognac and the stock. With the aid of a skimmer take out as many truffles as possible, but never mind if a few pieces stay in the sauce. Mix the skimmed truffles with the eggs and beat again. Make the omelette, place it in a deep porcelain dish and pour the sauce over it. Serve.

THE PREPARATION
AND USE OF THE
CLASSIC SAUCES

ESPAGNOLE SAUCE

For many years, despite its present decline in popularity, this sauce held its place as the great foundation brown sauce. It is therefore reasonable to consider critically both the methods of cooking and of employing such a sauce.

Short cuts must be eliminated and not a single error permitted. It is only on this condition that such sauces can reveal their true excellence and therefore survive.

If we examine the transformations undergone by sauce espagnole during some two hundred years, we shall no doubt be surprised, but I do not think that it has in fact degenerated.

I have chosen some examples in chronological order, but feel it is unnecessary to cite too many authorities. I have taken one example from *Les Soupers de la Cour*, 1755; one from *Le Nouveau Cuisinier Royal et Bourgeois*, Massialot, 1758, another from *L'Art de la Cuisine Française* by Carême, 1835, one from Durand's *Le Cuisinier* published in 1837, and one from Escoffier, 1921. It is noteworthy that with the exception of Dubois and Bernard, who gave a very complicated recipe in their book *La Cuisine Classique*, published in 1856, the others are all very similar. Durand gives in addition variations of several recipes for espagnole – an economical one, a 'bourgeois' recipe and one which includes both poultry and game. In the *Cuisine Classique* the authors have clearly piled Ossa upon Pelion. The sauce was made in four stages which included the addition of saddle of hare and partridge carcasses after the absorption of ham, knuckle of veal, sides of beef and poultry. It was moistened with Champagne, white wine, meat gravies and finally, clear soup, and was very far from the somewhat cold austerity of Escoffier. Vincent de la Chapelle, in the eighteenth century, while being true to his time and sacrificing ham, veal, beef, Champagne, herbs and spices, had points in common with ourselves today.

However, one no longer makes an espagnole in the way described by Escoffier and, naturally, we never use prefabricated roux. Whilst on the subject, I should like to say a little more about roux. Formerly, this would be prepared in advance, in quite large quantities, poured onto shallow trays to cool, and then cut in small pieces which were used as need arose. They were stored in metal boxes and hermetically sealed.

Although I am in agreement with my father's methods, I will give a recipe for espagnole which will be completely satisfactory today. Some changes in the ingredients of a foundation sauce must be accepted; the richness of the larder must be the cook's guide.

In his preface Escoffier lays down what he held to be a basic essential, the necessity for sauce cooks to have available the whole range of ingredients necessary to good cooking. I, too, have always been convinced of this.

SAUCE POIVRADE

Put a piece of butter in a casserole along with some slices of onion, some carrot and parsnip grated, a little basil, 2 cloves of garlic and 2 cloves and half a parsley root; cook and strain when it has begun to colour. Moisten with some *coulis*, half a glass of vinegar, some stock, salt and pepper; boil and reduce until it becomes just the right thickness for a sauce. Remove the fat and strain through a tammy cloth.

(*Les Soupers de la Cour*, 1755)

SAUCE APPELÉE POIVRADE

Put some vinegar in a pan with a little gravy, a whole shallot and an onion cut in slices; add a slice of lemon and season with salt and pepper. Boil, taste and make sure that the taste is good. Strain through a sieve, pour into a sauceboat and serve.

(*Le Nouveau Cuisinier Royal et Bourgeois*, Massialot, 1758)

SAUCE POIVRADE

Put 2 chopped onions and carrots into a stewpan; add a little lean ham, sprigs of parsley, some thyme, bay leaves, a good pinch of coarse pepper and a little mace. Then add 2 tablespoonfuls of good vinegar and the same of consommé. Simmer this seasoning over a very low fire. When it is reduced, add 2 more tablespoonfuls of consommé and 2 of prepared espagnole. After boiling for a short time, strain the sauce and rub it through a strainer. Reduce until it is just right. Just before serving, add a little butter.

The addition of the chopped carrots and onions gives more flavour; the sweetness of these root vegetables counterbalances the sharpness of the sauce. In this recipe, as in many others, I have followed the example of the celebrated Laguipierre. Whenever a sauce seemed too sharp to the palate, he added a touch of sugar to counteract this.

(*L'Art de la Cuisine Française*, Carême, 1835)

SAUCE ESPAGNOLE TRAVAILLÉE AU FUMET DE VOLAILLE ET DE GIBIER

Take care to use a lined saucepan, for this helps to make the sauce glisten. Put in some chicken or game stock, according to the type of entrée you are going to serve. Add some espagnole sauce and leave on the corner of the stove; skim and remove the fat; return to the fire and keep stirring until the sauce is ready. Then strain it.

When you are using game stock, add half a glass of Madeira and some truffles.

(*Le Cuisinier*, Durand, 1837)

SAUCE ESPAGNOLE

1 lb. roux
16 pints (20 pints) brown
  stock
mirepoix
6 oz. diced bacon
8 oz. carrots
6 oz. onions
3 sprigs thyme
2 small bay leaves

Bring about three-quarters of the stock to the boil; add the roux, previously softened and stir in with a spatula or a whisk. Bring up to the boil again and continue to cook slowly and gently just at boiling point.

Now prepare the *mirepoix*. Melt the fat in a *sauteuse*. Add the carrot and onion, cut up in a *brunoise*, the thyme and bay leaves. Sauté until the vegetables are lightly coloured. Carefully pour off the fat and then add the vegetables to the sauce. Deglaze the pan with a glass of white wine. Reduce the volume of the sauce by half and simmer gently for 1 hour, skimming the surface frequently.

Strain the sauce through a conical sieve, rubbing the vegetables lightly. Add the remainder of the stock and boil for another 2 hours slowly and regularly.

Finally, strain the sauce into a bowl
and leave until it is quite cold.
(*Le Guide Culinaire*, A. Escoffier, 1921)

The preparation of frugal and plain dishes in the seventeenth and
eighteenth centuries is obscure and hard to clarify. Certain foods remain
hallowed by tradition and others have fallen completely into disuse. We
owe these recipes to the practical requirements of religious feast days.
They are not of much interest today. In the preparation of such dishes,
known as *aliments maigres*, fish stock replaced meat stock.

Demi-glace. A highly concentrated espagnole. It was considered quite
good enough formerly to skin, strain and restrain it. Today a *demi-glace*
is classified as a good quality sauce with an espagnole or veal stock base.
It has practically disappeared, and we are really clinging to a word rather
than a recipe.

ESPAGNOLE SAUCE

celery
turnips
fresh fennel
white and green leeks
ham fat
lard
sauce:
flour
water
white wine
mixed herbs
roast onion
5-6 cloves
parsley

Sauté all the *mirepoix* ingredients in a
heavy copper-bottomed and enamelled
saucepan or a fireproof casserole. When
the vegetables are soft and a pale golden
colour, sprinkle flour over them and then
sauté a few more minutes till the flour is
similarly coloured. Moisten with water,
white wine or clear stock. Bring to the
boil and add a bone from a smoked ham,
a shin of veal and a shin of beef. These
bones must have flesh and tendons still
on them. Add herbs - parsley, chervil,
thyme, bay leaf, rosemary - the roasted
but not overcooked onion, stuck with 5
or 6 cloves, salt and pepper. Bring to the
boil, and when it is boiling nicely, skim;
cover, put in the oven and leave to cook
slowly for 3 hours at least. Take out and
strain through a clean tammy cloth.
Return to the fire, bring to the boil once

more and strain through a fine conical strainer into a glass or porcelain bowl. Leave this to cool, stirring from time to time with a wooden spoon. Use this sauce, as required, for various dishes, e.g. braised sweetbreads with sherry, or pepper steak.

BRAISED SWEETBREADS IN SHERRY (*Ris de Veau Braisés au Xérès*)

set of calves' sweetbreads
wineglassful of sherry
salt
pepper
prepared espagnole sauce
croûtons of bread
knob of butter

Soak the sweetbreads in cold water, blanch and skin them, place between plates or boards. Dust with flour, season with salt and pepper. Brown all over in a mixture of hot oil and butter. Drain off the fat (this will not be used again in the cooking). Add a wineglassful of sherry, brown gently and let it evaporate. Pour a generous dash of espagnole over the sweetbreads and put the uncovered pan in a warm oven. Every 5 or 6 minutes turn the sweetbreads and baste with the sauce. Add a little more of the espagnole, but do not overdo it. The sweetbreads will be ready in 20 minutes.

Take the sweetbreads out of the pan and place them on croûtons of bread in the serving dish. Keep them warm. Now strain the sauce through a conical strainer into a clean casserole or stewpan, stretch it with a little more sherry, scraping clean the bottom of the pan with, if needed, a little more sherry. Bring to the boil, take away from the fire, make the sauce perfectly smooth with a knob of good butter. Cover the sweetbreads with the sauce, garnish and serve.

Braised Sweetbreads au gratin (*Gratin de Ris de Veau à la Madras*)

CASSEROLE OF DUCK WITH GREEN PEPPER (*Capilotade de Canard au Poivre Vert*)

Illustrating the use of a brown sauce.

6 servings:

2 ducks (about 3 lb. each)
4 fl. oz. (½ cup) oil
1 oz. butter
24 little onions
6 cloves garlic
2 oz. flour
1 bottle dry white wine
10 oz. green pepper, fresh or canned
6 tomatoes
bouquet garni
water

Cut up the ducks into 6 pieces each. Put oil and butter into a *cocotte*. Heat it and leave the pieces to simmer gently. Prepare the onions and garlic. Once the pieces of duck have achieved a pale colour, even on all sides, withdraw them and reserve. Into the *cocotte* put the little onions and the garlic and allow them gently to take colour. Sprinkle over them the flour and allow it to cook gently. Add the wine (such as Pouilly Fumé or a medium-dry Graves). Add the green pepper. It is worth noting that one needs a lot of green pepper not because it has any flavouring power, but because of its aroma. Bring to the boil while stirring the bottom of the vessel with a wooden spoon to prevent the sauce from sticking. Add the tomatoes, peeled and cored, a bouquet garni and enough water to make the sauce fairly clear on the one hand and on the other to cover the pieces of duck which you now replace in the *cocotte*. Cook gently with the cover on for about 1 hour 15 minutes.

It is very important to judge the quantity of liquid carefully. In theory the quantities of wine and water should be about the same, but the quality and consistency of the sauce will depend as much on this as on the actual time of the cooking and the amount of liquid will depend in part on the size of the tomatoes.

Casserole of Duck with Green Peppers (*Capilotade de Canard au Poivre Vert*)

PEPPER STEAK (*Steak au Poivre*)
per serving:

6-8 oz. fillet or rump steak
peppercorns
1 tablespoonful of lard
salt
4 tablespoonfuls Cognac or young Armagnac
½ glass port
small soupladleful of espagnole sauce

Rub coarsely-ground pepper, or peppercorns, generously all over an uncooked fillet or rump steak. Force the pepper hard into the surface of the meat so that it will adhere to it. Meanwhile warm a tablespoonful of lard (not vegetable oil), not too much, but just enough to cover the bottom of the pan, which should be a heavy frying pan or *sauteuse* (a pan halfway between a frying pan and a saucepan). As soon as the lard is hot, salt the meat; this should be done at the last possible moment, then quickly seal the steak on both sides in the fat. This manoeuvre should be done extremely quickly if you wish the pepper to stick to the steak. Leave until you have reached the degree of cooking required. Do not turn the steak above 2 or 3 times.

Drain the fat from the pan. Add 4 tablespoonfuls of Cognac or young Armagnac. Light it and leave it to die down, then add ½ glass port and a small soupladleful of espagnole sauce. Take the steak out and put it on the warmed serving dish. Reduce the sauce a little, strain, take off the fire, add a knob of butter, stir it in and serve.

SOME VARIATIONS OF ESPAGNOLE SAUCE

AIGRE-DOUCE
A French version of the Italian *agro-dolce* (*see* Bitter-sweet sauces, page 96). It is served with small cuts of meat of giblets. Sugar, vinegar, shallots, wine, raisins and capers are added to the basic espagnole sauce.

BIGARADE

For roast duck and game. An orange sauce using fine strips of marmalade oranges, orange and lemon juice and seasoning.

BORDELAISE

(*See* page 96.)

BOURGUIGNONNE

A variant of *sauce Bordelaise* in which a red Burgundy is used instead of the Bordeaux. It should be more highly seasoned.

CHAMBERTIN

Another variant of *sauce Bordelaise*, simply substituting Chambertin for the ordinary Burgundy used in *sauce Bourguignonne*.

CHARCUTIÈRE

For grilled or fried pork. *Demi-glace* sauce is added to fried chopped onions, and then chopped gherkins; vinegar or mustard may be stirred in before serving.

CHASSEUR

A variation of *Genevoise* (*q.v.*) in which the sauce is made from the liquid used to cook the fish, with red wine added as well, for small cuts of meat, sautéed chicken or game birds. Mushrooms, chopped shallots, white wine, tomato sauce, butter and herbs are added to an espagnole sauce.

CHATEAUBRIAND

This sauce was formerly served with Chateaubriand steaks, but *sauce Béarnaise* is now used instead. It was made by adding white wine and chopped shallots to espagnole sauce; lemon juice, chopped tarragon and cayenne pepper were used as seasoning.

CHAUD-FROID

Brown *chaud-froid* may be used to coat various cold brown meats. There are variants for duck and game. For fish, chicken and tomato *chaud-froid see* velouté sauce (page 71) and for eggs and hors d'oeuvre, use thick mayonnaise with a little gelatine.

CHEVREUIL

For venison. A variation of *sauce poivrade* which has red wine and a *mirepoix* of vegetables added to it together with finely cut up pieces of cooked venison.

COLBERT

For grills, meat and vegetables. Meat or fish glaze, light stock, softened butter are mixed and seasoned with lemon juice, Madeira and parsley.

DIABLE

Chopped shallots, vinegar, white wine and fresh herbs are incorporated into a base of *demi-glace* espagnole. If a tomato *demi-glace* is substituted as well as a dash of Worcester sauce, *sauce diable* becomes devilled sauce. These variations are served with grilled meat.

FINANCIÈRE

For sweetbreads, vol-au-vent and poultry. Use chicken stock, truffles and mushrooms and Sauternes or Madeira with the basic espagnole.

GENEVOISE

This sauce is most commonly served with trout and salmon. A fish espagnole is added to a *mirepoix* of vegetables and fish stock; red wine, anchovy essence and butter are incorporated. *Sauce Génoise* is an old name for *sauce Genevoise* and is now practically obsolete.

GODARD

For sweetbreads and poultry. Raw ham, carrots, onions, Champagne and mushrooms are used to lengthen the espagnole sauce.

GRAND VENEUR

For venison. The ingredients are *sauce poivrade* with gooseberry jelly, and if liked, thick cream and hare's blood.

LYONNAISE

This is a very useful sauce for left-over meat, ragoûts, and braised meat. It is basically an onion sauce with white wine, wine vinegar, butter, blended with the espagnole.

MADÈRE

For braised or roast meat, mostly in small cuts. Madeira, stock, gravy, butter and concentrated espagnole sauce are its constituents.

MUSHROOM

Suitable for use with chicken, fish and meat. Use whichever stock is appropriate for the recipes, sliced mushrooms, wine and butter as well.

PÉRIGUEUX

One of the most famous of the classical sauces, it may be served with small cuts of meat, chicken or game. It consists of diced truffles and Madeira blended into a *demi-glace* espagnole sauce. A further variation is called *sauce Périgourdine*, the only difference being that the truffles are cut in thick rounds instead of being diced.

POIVRADE

This famous sauce can be used for any number of dishes but principally for grilled meat and ragoûts. It is important to remember that it is much better to add the pepper at the later stages of preparation as too much pepper cooked slowly for a long time will taste bitter and the hot peppery flavour, set off by vegetable and herbs and sharpened by the vinegar, will be lost. The ingredients can vary according to the dish – for instance, use giblets and a little marinade for game recipes, or meat glaze is a possibility instead of espagnole, or red wine instead of white. Generally speaking, however, the ingredients are wine vinegar, white wine, peppercorns, a *mirepoix* of vegetables, bay leaf, thyme, light stock and espagnole sauce. If the sauce is flavoured with game essense and blended with butter and cream, it becomes *sauce Diane. Sauce Moscovite* is the same sauce with juniper berries and a glass of Malaga or Marsala added.

REFORM

Reform sauce is simply a garnished *sauce poivrade* served with mutton chops or lamb cutlets. Gherkins, sliced hard-boiled white of egg, cooked mushrooms, a little chopped salt or pickled tongue and a truffle are all cut up small and added at the last minute. It was created by Alexis Soyer when he was chef at the Reform Club in London about 1830.

ROBERT
This is one of the oldest of all the surviving sauces of the past. Chopped onion, a roux, meat stock or consommé make up its ingredients with vinegar and mustard as the seasoning.

ROMAINE
Sugar lumps are dissolved in vinegar and added to a reduced espagnole with game stock. A final touch is the addition of pine kernels and some raisins and sultanas.

VÉRON
For fish. Wine and herbs prepared as for *sauce Béarnaise* are mixed with *sauce Normande* and concentrated fish *fumet*. The seasoning is heightened with cayenne and chopped chervil and tarragon.

BÉCHAMEL SAUCE

Traditionally, béchamel is attributed to Louis de Béchameil, Marquis de Nointel, who made his fortune during the Fronde, that rising of nobles and *Parlement* against the regency of Cardinal Mazarin which began in 1648 and lasted until 1653. It was at this time that the young Louis XIV was forced by his mother and the Cardinal to display himself to the rebels as he lay in bed, rigid with fear and disgust, in the palace of the Louvre. This episode was commonly supposed to have given him a life-long dislike of Paris.

The Marquis de Nointel became Lord Steward to Louis's household. The sauce is believed to have been introduced by him or his chef, but may merely have been dedicated to him.

The method of making béchamel has changed, for even as late as the time of Carême, in the nineteenth century, béchamel was made by stirring generous quantities of cream into a velouté sauce. Today the method is different, and the ingredients are butter, flour and milk, all of the best and creamiest quality.

There are, even so, two methods possible for the basic preparation, the ingredients and their proportions remaining the same. *Either* make a light roux in the proportions of 1½–2 oz. butter, the same or a little more of flour, to ½ pint (1¼ cups) of milk, and then incorporate the milk which should be boiling; be very careful to avoid lumps, season with salt, pepper and a little grated nutmeg. *Or* take the butter, melt it, and when it is sizzling, blend in the flour and then carefully and slowly add the milk (which should in this case be cold) little by little, until it is all blended and the sauce is quite smooth and without lumps. Continue cooking and stirring until the sauce thickens. Season with salt, pepper and a little grated nutmeg as above. If the ultimate disaster of lumps does happen, press or rub the sauce through a fine sieve and return to the pan to reheat, or give a few turns in the electric blender.

Béchamel may be made before it is needed for use and stored in the refrigerator. It can be varied in many ways according to your recipe. Hard-boiled eggs, chopped parsley, mushrooms, oysters, shrimps, to name only a few. For richness, stir in yolk of egg; for piquancy, a little lemon juice.

BÉCHAMEL AU NATUREL

Take half a litre of double cream and boil it, stirring all the while until it is reduced by more than half and is thickened like an ordinary sauce. Take sliced breast of chicken which has been roasted on a spit and then left to grow cold, and put it into the sauce a moment before serving, so that it warms through without boiling. Season with salt and coarse pepper and serve.

(*La Nouvelle Cuisine*, 1751)

SAUCE À LA CREME, COMMUNEMENT APPELÉE BÉCHAMEL

Pour into a saucepan, the amount being according to the quantity of sauce you need, light veal stock or meat stock, which also has little colour. Season with salt, spices, some shallots, a clove of garlic, half a bay leaf, a sprig of blanched tarragon, some parsley and chives. Let this come to the boil and remove from the fire, and do this several times. Strain into another pan through a cloth. Add a piece of good butter well rolled in flour, and then some sweet fresh cream or in place of this milk which you have boiled previously. Stir this sauce over a fire until it is blended and serve.

If the sauce does not have enough body, you may remedy this by adding
one or two yolks of eggs.

(Traité Historique et Pratique de la Cuisine, 1758)

GRANDE SAUCE BÉCHAMEL EN MAIGRE

Cut fillets of a medium sized brill, previously skinned, into small slices.
Put in a large (unsalted) sauté pan with 12 oz. of unsalted butter, 2 onions,
2 carrots, 16 mushrooms and 4 roots of parsley, all chopped. Add a scrap of
bay leaf, some thyme and basil, mace, a pinch of coarse pepper and grated
nutmeg. Heat over a moderate fire, mixing the seasoning with a wooden
spoon for 10 minutes. Add 2 large spoonfuls of flour, which you must mix
very thoroughly, and little by little 3 pints of cream. Do not leave the
béchamel but reduce on a moderate fire for some 20-25 minutes. Then
press through a tammy cloth and pour into a terrine.

(Art de la Cuisine Française, Carême, 1835)

SAUCE BÉCHAMEL À L'ESSENCE DE CHAMPIGNON

Put about a pint of béchamel into a saucepan with 4 oz. of mushroom
essence. Reduce to a quarter of its original volume and strain through a
sieve. Just before serving add 4 oz. of butter, a little nutmeg and 2 large
spoonfuls of double cream. Concentrated chicken stock, the liquid in
which truffles have been cooked, or fish stock may be used. It may be
served as a rich sauce or a plain one for fast days.

(La Cuisine Classique, Urbain Dubois and E. Bernard, 1856)

SAUCE BÉCHAMEL

Put into a small stockpot a shin or knuckle of veal, a chicken and the white
vegetables, leeks, celery, you have ready, and 6 oz. of raw blanched ham.
Moisten with about 8-10 pints of water. Start boiling, skim, add an onion,
a carrot, a bouquet garni, several cloves, and some peppercorns. Draw to
the corner of the stove and leave to simmer just at boiling point. Prepare
a roux with 1 lb. of butter and $\frac{3}{4}$ lb. flour. When it is ready, strain the
bouillon in the stockpot, remove the fat, and mix a little into the roux.
When half of the bouillon has been absorbed, place the pan on the fire,
bring the sauce to the boil without ceasing to stir with the wooden spoon
so that it will blend without being lumpy. The first time it boils, add the
rest of the bouillon until it is liquid. Then draw the pan off the fire to the

corner of the stove and let it simmer for three-quarters of an hour. Remove the skin and continue the cooking for another 20 minutes; then strain through a tammy cloth into another saucepan for the reduction. Place this pan in a hot oven and reduce the sauce by a third. At this stage incorporate slowly $1\frac{3}{4}$ pints ($2\frac{1}{4}$ pints) of double cream, never ceasing the stirring, which ought to be more vigorous. When the cream is absorbed, strain again into a terrine, fan until it is half cold, then cover with a round of paper. The same sauce is made by mixing cream with a reduced velouté. This method is the shortest but not the most perfect.

(*La Cuisine Classique*, Urbain Dubois et E. Bernard, 1856)

BRAISED SWEETBREADS AU GRATIN (*Gratin de Ris de Veau à la Madras*)

Illustrating the use of a white sauce.

6 servings:

3 pairs sweetbreads of about 2 lb. the pair
2 lb. onions
5 oz. shallots
1 carrot
$\frac{1}{2}$ bottle dry white wine
water as needed
salt, cayenne, nutmeg
bouquet garni
2 oz. ($\frac{1}{4}$ cup) flour
2 oz. ($\frac{1}{4}$ cup) Dutch cheese
2 oz. ($\frac{1}{4}$ cup) Gruyère
1 oz. Parmesan
for the liaison:
3 dessertspoonfuls curry
6 dessertspoonfuls powdered milk
3 egg yolks
juice of 2 lemons
5 oz. (over $\frac{1}{2}$ cup) butter
3 fl. oz. (almost $\frac{1}{2}$ cup) oil
flour as required

Place the sweetbreads in some large receptacle, cover them generously with water, add a little salt and bring to the boil. Boil for 2 or 3 minutes, then withdraw from the heat, empty the water and place the sweetbreads in running cold water for 10–15 minutes. Withdraw them and pat them dry in a cloth. Peel them so that all skin and adhesions are removed. Flour them and colour them in a *cocotte* or a large casserole, using 3 oz. oil, 3 oz. butter. Use a gentle heat so that they take colour without the mixture of oil and butter turning black. During this process add salt and pepper lightly and then reserve them on a hot plate. In the same saucepan repeat the process with the vegetables which will have been peeled and coarsely chopped. After they have taken a little colour add flour, continue cooking for a little and then add the white wine and an equal quantity of water. Add the bouquet garni, salt, pepper and nut-meg and put the sweetbreads back to cook. Bring them to the boil and let them simmer for 45 minutes. Dry the sweet-breads. Pass the sauce through muslin or strain through a fine sieve. Bring it to the boil again, then bind it with the powdered milk, the curry powder, the egg yolks, the lemon juice and a little water to ensure a fluid consistency.

Bring the sauce to the boil and keep it boiling for 2 or 3 minutes, beating it the whole time. Set the sweetbreads in an ovenproof dish, pour quarter of the hot sauce round them; pour the balance of it over the top of them. Sprinkle the dish with the mixture of the three grated cheeses and spread the remaining 2 oz. of butter in small shreds over the top. Place the dish in a medium oven for 20 minutes. Serve with Créole rice or jacket potatoes.

BRAISED AUBERGINES AND COURGETTES AU GRATIN (*Gratin Albigeois*)
Illustrating an unusual use of a béchamel sauce.
6 servings:

$\frac{3}{4}$ **lb. tomatoes**
$\frac{3}{4}$ **lb. aubergines (egg plant)**
$\frac{3}{4}$ **lb. courgettes**
2 fl. oz. ($\frac{1}{4}$ cup) oil
2 oz. ($\frac{1}{4}$ cup) butter
2 pints (2$\frac{1}{2}$ pints) milk
4 oz. ($\frac{1}{2}$ cup) grated Gruyère

After cleaning and peeling the vegetables, slice and cook each one separately and briskly in 2 fl. oz. oil and 2 oz. butter.

Prepare a béchamel according to the classic method (*see* page 57), using 2 pints milk boiled for 20 minutes with salt, nutmeg, thyme, and bay leaf, and then blended into a light roux made of 4 oz. butter and 4 oz. flour. Cook the sauce for a few minutes. In a gratin dish set a layer of béchamel, then a layer of courgettes, then more béchamel, then the tomatoes, then more béchamel, then the aubergines and finally the last of the béchamel over the top. Sprinkle over this the grated Gruyère and finish in the oven.

SMOKED SALMON SOUFFLÉ (*Soufflé de Saumon Fumé*)
Illustrating the use of *sauce Mornay*.

6 servings:

12 eggs

1 lb. smoked salmon, chopped small

1 pint (1¼ pints) ordinary sauce Mornay

4 oz. (½ cup) butter to grease the soufflé moulds

2 oz. grated Gruyère

Grease 2 soufflé moulds generously and then sprinkle the grated cheese in them.

Place the smoked salmon, the egg yolks and 5 tablespoonfuls of the sauce into a mixing bowl and give the mixture a quick whirl with the electric mixer so as to achieve a homogeneous consistency. Mix in thoroughly the rest of the sauce. Beat the whites of eggs until they are very stiff and fold them into the prepared mixture. Put in a medium oven and cook gently for 30–40 minutes.

SOME VARIATIONS OF BÉCHAMEL SAUCE

AURORE
For egg and poultry dishes. A béchamel coloured pink with paprika.

À LA CRÈME
For eggs, fish, poultry and vegetables. Either a béchamel reduced and with fresh cream and butter beaten in at the last moment, or a white roux with cream incorporated instead of the usual milk for béchamel sauce. This variant is usually served with roast veal.

CARDINAL

For fish. Fish *fumet* and béchamel are warmed together. Cream, poached lobster or lobster butter and cayenne pepper are added. Truffles also may be included.

ÉCOSSAISE

For eggs, poultry, sweetbreads, brains. A variation of sauce *à la crème* for which a *brunoise* of vegetables is added as well as diced French beans.

MORNAY

For chicken, eggs, fish and vegetables. A cheese béchamel with many uses. Gruyère is most often used for *sauce Mornay*, finely grated, or Parmesan if preferred. Use chicken, fish or vegetable stock according to the dish, or cream if liked. This sauce is very often employed for dishes au gratin.

NANTUA

For fish, shellfish or eggs. *Sauce Nantua* and dishes *Nantua* imply the use of crayfish in their preparation. Fish *fumet*, cream, a *mirepoix* of vegetables, crayfish purée and béchamel sauce are its constituents. White wine or a little brandy, or tomato purée or fresh tomatoes are also permissible.

POULETTE

For mussels, veal or vegetables. A béchamel moistened with stock or the liquid of the dish for which the sauce is intended. Add cream and egg yolks, lemon juice and seasoning.

SHRIMP SAUCE OR SAUCE AUX CREVETTES

For fish. Boiled, peeled shrimps are added to a rich béchamel with thick cream as well. The heads may be pounded in a mortar and sieved before adding to the sauce.

SOUBISE

For eggs, roast pork, chicken or mutton. It is basically a purée of onions with béchamel, and chicken bouillon or veal stock. Nutmeg adds point to the seasoning.

VELOUTÉ SAUCE

The importance of veloutés is ever increasing. They justify the present tendency to dispense with the use of *fond* (light stock). This is a return to the principle that the essential components of each dish must be contained in the sauce which is to accompany it.

Let us examine a characteristic example, the *blanquette*. Whatever the method selected, and however carefully the dish is prepared, it is all wasted if a light stock is used for moistening. Do not let us exaggerate too much, however. I do not think that moistening a *blanquette* with a very good quality stock would be contrary to the rules of good cooking. I simply think that these two constituents would jar. The saying that better is the enemy of best would be well proven here. A *blanquette* which preserves the bouquet of its herbs and the flavour of its meat, together with a rich smoothness of texture, will have my approval much more than one laced with meat glaze and thickened with cream.

The distinction between a velouté and a béchamel is a fine one. Substitute the liquid in which you have been cooking your dish (or chicken, veal stock or fish *fumet*) for the milk added to the roux and the béchamel becomes a velouté. In fact such a sauce was formerly known as a *béchamel grasse*.

The principle that cold milk is added to hot roux and vice versa must be repeated here. It is applicable to béchamel and velouté alike both in their basic and elaborated forms.

Sauce suprême is a highly sophisticated cream velouté and stands in the same relation to it as a *demi-glace* to an espagnole. In fact, all veloutés should be *suprêmes*. It is unforgivable not to finish a job begun with so much labour.

There are two classes of basic veloutés: meat and fish. Of the meat veloutés, two are of the first importance: chicken and veal, which are both white meats. Fish veloutés are made from deep water fish such as sole, turbot and John Dory, which all make the very delicate *fumets* or fish stocks for the best veloutés. The golden rule for making a *fumet* is – never reduce. It should not be cooked slowly, nor for a long time, and it should be used as quickly as it is made. If it is reduced, this must be done very quickly indeed, which is very difficult and is properly the province of professional cooks. It is of major importance to have small volume *fumets* from the start.

I have already explained that reduction is necessary before blending. In simple terms, if you need a pint of sauce, and a pint only, you must so arrange it that the fish stock plus the blending ingredient will not exceed this quantity. The constituents of the latter, cream, egg yolks and butter or any combination of these three, are bland in relation to the main flavour. It is obviously necessary for the stock to have sufficient flavour for the whole. Because of this there is a tendency on the part of chefs to reduce *fumets*, but this is only feasible for professionals, as their knowledge of the material and their skill, minimize the risk. Even a skilful and experienced amateur runs a serious risk of reducing the stock too slowly, thereby losing the initial flavour. Slowly made fish stocks retain the taste of fatty fish (herring, mackerel, sardines); blending certainly diminishes this, but not entirely. *Fumets* should therefore be planned to be very rich in fish so as to avoid the necessity for reduction.

There are recipes for all occasions. *Blanquette* and fish sauce are two basic examples. Chicken *blanquette* can be made in two ways, *à l'ancienne* and *en fricassée*. The main difference between the two lies in the liquid, which in the first method is clear and in the second thick.

CHICKEN FRICASSÉE (*Blanquette de Volaille en Fricassée*)

For this dish there is a choice of two methods, either using vegetables and water, or a light stock. The beginning of the preparations will be different.

Cut up the chicken, flour the pieces and sauté in a mixture of butter and oil. Colour them lightly. Put on one side and add the vegetables to the same fat. When the vegetables have taken colour, replace the chicken, dust with flour and add the liquid. Add a bouquet garni and leave to cook. This will take longer than does the *blanquette à l'ancienne*. Then remove the meat, strain, blend and garnish in the same way as for the previous recipe. What happens, in fact, is that the cooking is done in the sauce instead of in a clear bouillon thickened at the end of the cooking. The same garnishes are used – pastas, spaghetti, *lasagne*, macaroni can all be used. I prefer not to have a mountain of garnishes and would prefer to omit the mushrooms and baby onions if I were having potatoes or *tagliatelle*.

OLD-FASHIONED CHICKEN STEW (*Blanquette de Volaille à l'ancienne, Oliver Père*)

mirepoix:
onions
carrots
turnips
celery
leeks
little garlic

1 chicken
bouquet garni
a few cloves
zest of a lemon
water
salt
coarse mignonette pepper
½-1 oz. flour
½-1 oz. butter
1 pint (1¼ pints) clear stock
2 yolks of eggs
juice of small lemon
4 fl. oz. (½ cup) double cream
tiny onions
mushrooms

Fry the *mirepoix* in butter until it colours lightly, then add the meat cut in pieces, the bouquet garni, cloves and zest of lemon. Add the water. (The main difference between my father's method and that of Escoffier is that the latter used light stock and proceeded from there on, much as is done for a *pot-au-feu*, using carrots, onions stuck with cloves and so on.) Season with salt and a little mignonette pepper. Bring to the boil, strain and cook on a low heat until it is well done. This is most important. I have often said that this means virtually taking it to the point of its being overdone.

Take out the pieces of chicken and keep them hot in a pan with the merest breath of heat. Make a roux in the proportions of ½ oz. or 1 oz. each of flour and of butter to a pint of clear stock. Add the liquid while cooking the roux. Bring to the boil, and let it cook for a few minutes. Blend with 2 eggs to each pint of sauce, the juice of a small lemon, a little cayenne pepper, more salt if necessary and 4 fl. oz. (½ cup) double cream.

Contrary to general opinion, after the sauce is blended with the utmost care, boil it hard. This is to stabilize the sauce and make it smooth and creamy. Then pour over the chicken, bring to boiling point and keep hot. *Blanquette à l'ancienne* should be served garnished with tiny onions and mushrooms prepared in *court-bouillon*.

There are many other garnishes; pilaff of rice is becoming more and more common. Personally, I like nothing better than potatoes *en robe de chambre* (baked in their jackets).

FISH VELOUTÉ SAUCE

Fish *fumets* are discussed elsewhere (*see* page 36). There are two ways of approaching the problem; either the *fumet* is made from fish heads, tails and trimmings boiled in a mixture of three-quarters water and one-quarter white wine, or a *mirepoix* of vegetables is first gently stewed in butter and the fish heads and trimmings are then added, along with the water and wine in the same proportions as before. The amount of liquid depends on the quantity of the heads. Often a fish does not have enough odd pieces to make a good *fumet*, so it must be strengthened. For the professional cook, this presents no problem, as many filleted fish do not have their trimmings used for sauces and so there is always a surplus of bones which can be used to make the *fumet* up to strength. Usually one employs the heads of noble fish such as turbot, brill or John Dory, whole cod or whiting. Boil the fish in the stock, to which a little butter and some white wine is often added. This is the liquid which will be used for the sauce.

FILLETS OF SOLE IN WHITE WINE (*Filets de Sole au Vin Blanc*)

2 soles
water
wine
mirepoix **of vegetables**
butter
fresh herbs
2½-3 oz. flour
2½-3 oz. butter
egg yolks
double cream
lemon juice
salt, pepper

Skin and clean the soles. Fillet them and reserve the bones and trimmings. Fold and trim the fillets. Prepare the *fumet* according to one of the methods given above. Brown the vegetables in butter and season with salt and fresh herbs; boil for 10-15 minutes and then strain through a tammy cloth and then a sieve. This *fumet* is also used for the sauce.

Lay the fillets two per person on an ovenproof dish, either a glass or an enamel one, and cover with the *fumet* which should be either tepid or cold.

Fillets of Sole in White Wine (*Filets de Sole au Vin Blanc*)

Bring to the boil, draw off the fire and they will continue to cook for a few moments. The fish is then kept warm in the *fumet*.

Now prepare the sauce. Make a light roux in the proportions of $2\frac{1}{2}$ oz. butter to $2\frac{1}{2}$ oz. flour; the latter may be increased up to 3 oz. according to the quality of the flour. Add $1\frac{2}{3}$ pints ($2\frac{1}{4}$ pints) of *fumet*, boil and strain before blending. Certain rules must be observed. Do not reduce the sauce after it has been thickened. If the *fumet* requires reducing do this before it is added to the roux. This ought to be cold, and the *fumet* boiling or vice versa. The roux can be cooled by standing the saucepan in cold water. Blend with the egg yolks and cream and a little lemon juice; check for seasoning. The amount of egg yolk will vary according to the total quantity of sauce, roughly 1 egg yolk to each serving.

Fish velouté is usually served at large dinners or for multiple servings in a restaurant. If, however, only 2 or 4 fillets of sole are to be prepared the preparation given below is preferable, but only in skilled hands.

Butter a sauté pan and cover with a layer of finely-chopped shallots, season and lay the fillets of sole on top, add enough *fumet*, white wine and butter to cover the shallots. Cook the fish until it is done, lift out the fish and keep warm. Strain the liquid into a smaller saucepan. Reduce until all you have left is a thin coating in the bottom of the pan, then add

Braised Aubergines and Courgettes au gratin (*Gratin Albigeois*)

cream, enough but not too much. Bring
rapidly to the boil. Take off the flame and
add softened butter. Correct seasoning
and serve.

There are two tricks to be played when
using this method:

1. Add a little béchamel or *Mornay* sauce
   when reducing the sauce and before
   adding the cream. About a teaspoonful
   per person will be enough.
2. As a final touch add 1 dessertspoonful
   of hollandaise sauce to every 2 servings. This little bit of cheating is done
   by nearly all saucemakers.

SOME VARIATIONS OF VELOUTÉ SAUCE

BERCY

For fish and meat. A fish *fumet* is used for fish dishes and chicken stock or
meat glaze for meat recipes. Chopped shallots, sautéed in butter, are added
to velouté. Chopped parsley, white wine and butter are the other ingredients.

BRETONNE

For eggs, fish, white meat and poultry. A *julienne* of celery hearts, white
leeks and onions, mushrooms, white wine, butter and thick cream make
up the ingredients with, of course, a fish velouté for a fish recipe and
chicken velouté for a meat one. There is also a *sauce Bretonne* served with
meat which is not a variation of a velouté sauce, but is an onion sauce with
tomatoes or a tomato purée.

CHANTILLY

For eggs, poultry, sweetbreads and brains. There is also *sauce Chantilly*
which is a variation of mayonnaise and a béchamel sauce with cream may
also be known by this name. Velouté *Chantilly* is a variety of sauce
suprême in which thick cream is added to a very thick sauce. *Crème
Chantilly* is fresh whipped cream, sweetened and served as a sweet.

CHAUD-FROID

Velouté *chaud-froid* may be used for eggs, chicken, poultry and offal. Velouté sauce and mushroom *fumet* are blended with aspic, or chicken or veal jelly and cream to prepare this well-known sauce (*see also* cold emulsified and espagnole sauces and page 97).

CHAUD-FROID MAIGRE

For fish and shellfish. A fish velouté instead of a chicken or veal one and fish jelly in place of meat is the difference between *chaud-froid* and *chaud-froid maigre*. Other named varieties of the sauce are *chaud-froid à l'andalouse*, which has a sherry flavouring and strips of orange peel or a *julienne* of vegetables; *à l'aurore*, with tomato paste or concentrate added until the sauce is a rosy pink: *à la banquière* with chopped truffles and Madeira: *Beauharnais*, white *chaud-froid* coloured with tarragon and chervil: *à la Nantua*, a fish sauce with the addition of crayfish liquid.

CHIVRY

For eggs, fish, poultry. Velouté sauce with chervil and tarragon and other fresh herbs, white wine and chicken or fish stock.

DIPLOMATE OR RICHE

For fish. This is a variation of *sauce Normande* incorporating lobster butter, a little brandy and a pinch of cayenne, in addition to the ingredients for the *sauce Normande* (*q.v.*). Chopped truffles and lobster meat may also be folded in if the sauce is to be served separately in a sauceboat.

HONGROISE

For eggs, fish, sauté meat, poultry. Again the velouté should be based either on fish or chicken *fumet* or stock according to the recipe for which the sauce is destined. The ingredients are paprika powder, white wine, chopped onions, butter and a bouquet garni.

NORMANDE

For fish. This sauce has several variations the use of which depends on your mood, season and pocket. The basic ingredients are fish velouté sauce, fish *fumet*, concentrated mushroom stock, mussel or oyster liquor, egg yolks and cream. If you add truffles soaked in Madeira, or poached oysters, *sauce Normande* becomes *sauce Laguipière*. *Joinville* is basically the same as *Normande* with the further addition of sliced truffles. *Sauce Joinville* is used in conjunction with poultry.

RAVIGOTE
There are two *ravigote* sauces – a hot and a cold one. The cold one is a mayonnaise with capers and hard-boiled eggs, while the hot sauce is a very popular variation of velouté sauce. The hot *ravigote* is usually served with offal and poultry. It is made from a basic velouté roux moistened with vinegar and white wine and is seasoned with tarragon, thyme, bay leaves, parsley and mignonette pepper. Chopped onions or shallots and garlic are included according to the cook's discretion.

ROYALE
For poached eggs and boiled chicken. A concentrated velouté sauce is thinned with light chicken stock and given body with cream and stewed sieved truffles.

SUPRÊME
Sauce suprême is a chicken velouté with fresh thick double cream blended in at the last moment and fresh unsalted butter if liked. It is richer in taste than velouté and can be elaborated even further. For example, if Madeira is used with chopped truffles, it becomes *sauce banquière*. For *sauce Chantilly see* page 70. *Sauce ivoire* is a *suprême* with a little veal gravy or meat glaze to deepen the colour and give the sauce a meaty flavour.

TALLEYRAND
For poultry, pork and veal. This variation has cream, chicken or veal stock blended with the velouté sauce, and a *mirepoix* of vegetables, thick cream, Madeira and truffles and tongue cut up small in addition.

ALLEMANDE SAUCE

Sauce Allemande became *sauce Parisienne* after the Franco-Prussian war of 1870, just as Café Viennois changed to Café Liègeois during the First World War. It is spoken of as something legendary. In fact it is nothing more or less than a velouté. I give below, as an example, Escoffier's recipe. However, I have known a time when allemande was held to be a basic sauce and not, as Escoffier has said, a finished or compound sauce.

The disappearance of the word allemande from the culinary vocabulary is only superficial, for it can be said that the word is still in existence as everybody knows perfectly well to what it refers and for what stage of preparation. It will be enough to say during a discussion of the day's menus that, if a *Mornay* or a béchamel sauce will not do, an allemande must be prepared.

To make it, follow the general outline as laid down by my father for espagnole and simply omit the tomatoes. In every other respect the method is the same.

Although distinctions may be drawn we must admit that *sauce allemande* can nowadays be very easily confused with chicken velouté. In the hands of certain cooks who affect to despise béchamel (they call it 'glue') *sauce Allemande* gaily undertakes all the additional duties of béchamel, such as *Mornay* and *bâtarde*.

It is remarkable to note that in case of need it can even replace a fish velouté in the preparation of certain *coulis* which are already rich enough in marine aromas to absorb this adulteration.

Sauce Allemande is, virtually, no longer served as an accompaniment, but is very much used in the preparation of other composite sauces.

SAUCE À L'ALLEMANDE
Chop mushrooms, parsley, shallots, olives, cut some good slices of onions in butter, sprinkle with flour, add wine and bouillon; finish by grating a little Parmesan cheese; add a touch of vinegar and some breadcrumbs.

(*Les Dons de Comus*, 1739)

SAUCE VERTE POUR L'AGNEAU À L'ALLEMANDE

Take a fistful of green corn, a little one of sorrel, a blade or two of chives, a clove or two of shallots or else a slice of onion. Wash these and pound them adding a slice of toast soaked in vinegar. When everything is well pounded, put into a *casserole* together with a little sugar, a pinch of salt and a little Rhine wine. See to it that this sauce is bittersweet. It is the sauce-maker's duty to give it the right taste. However, take heed that the sugar does not predominate.

This sauce can also be served with poached eggs, when the dish may be named *Oeufs au vert-celadin*.

(*La Cuisinier Moderne*, Vincent de la Chapelle, 1742)

SAUCE À L'ALLEMANDE

Put a slice of ham in a pan, cook it till it is soft and moisten with bouillon and concentrated purée – bring it to the boil and reduce and remove the fat, strain through a sieve and add chopped and blanched parsley; chopped capers and anchovies, two shallots and two large pats of fresh Vambre butter. Blend the sauce over the fire, but do not let it become too thick. Remove the shallots and add some coarsely ground pepper and the juice of a lemon.

(*La Nouvelle Cuisine*, 1757)

SAUCE ALLEMANDE

To some prepared velouté sauce, you will put two or three egg yolks, according to the amount of sauce you require. When this is blended toss in a lump of fine butter about the size of half an egg: when the butter is melted stir into the sauce, strain through a cloth to get rid of any lumps. Keep the sauce hot in a *bain-marie*, add coarse pepper and make sure that it is properly salted.

(*Le Cuisinier Royal*, Viard, 1832)

SAUCE ALLEMANDE

Put $\frac{3}{4}$ pint of velouté sauce in a saucepan suitable for reducing; add 3 fl. oz. of chicken consommé and a spoonful of mushroom extract. Place this over a fierce heat and reduce using a spatula without splashing or letting the sauce stick to the pan. When the volume is reduced by two thirds, more or less, blend in two or three eggs with the further addition of 2 dessertspoonfuls of cold consommé and the juice of a lemon. Add a touch of nutmeg, bring to the boil once and then strain through a cloth. At the last moment, finish off the sauce with 3 oz. of butter.

By adding a spoonful of chopped and blanched parsley, this becomes old style *sauce poulette!*

(*La Cuisine Classique*, Urban Dubois et E. Bernard, 1856)

SAUCE PARISIENNE, FORMERLY *ALLEMANDE*

to make $1\frac{3}{4}$ pints ($2\frac{1}{4}$ pints):

$1\frac{3}{4}$ **pints ($2\frac{1}{4}$ pints) ordinary velouté sauce, blended with yolks of eggs**

5 yolks of eggs

18 fl. oz. ($2\frac{1}{4}$ cups) cold light stock

pinch of coarse mignonette pepper

grated nutmeg

3 oz. cooked mushrooms

little lemon juice

3 oz. fresh butter

Put all together in a thick-bottomed *sautoir* the mushrooms, stock, yolks of eggs, pepper, nutmeg and lemon juice. Mix everything with a whisk. Add the velouté; bring to the boil and cook till the sauce is reduced by a third, cooking hard and stirring the whole time with a spatula. Continue reducing until the mixture clings to the spoon and then strain it through a cloth. Slip a lump of butter on the surface which will prevent skin forming, and then keep hot in a *bain-marie*. At the last moment, just before using the sauce, add the butter as the final touch.

Note : we have substituted the name 'Parisienne' for 'Allemande', the latter being unjustifiable and its continued use only retained as a matter of habit, despite its obvious illogicality. M. Tavernet, in *L'Art Culinaire*, published in 1883, himself a talented practitioner, denounces this illogical habit. The nomenclature 'Parisienne' was adopted by several chefs, but not as generally as would have been desirable.

(*Le Guide Culinaire*, A. Escoffier, 1929)

SOME VARIATIONS OF ALLEMANDE SAUCE

Many of the variations for velouté sauce can be further altered by substituting allemande sauce for the velouté foundation.

BRANDADE

For boiled fish, especially associated with boiled salt cod (*morue*). It is a fish allemande with the addition of yolks of eggs, nutmeg, lemon juice blended with the sauce when it is cold. Olive oil is beaten into this mixture and finally some lemon juice.

MORILLES

For chicken. An old variation. Carême gives a recipe which uses rosemary, sage, thyme, basil (the most aromatic of herbs), bay leaf, cloves, nutmeg and mignonette pepper and chopped onions, as well as the *morilles*. Allemande sauce was added when these ingredients had been gently simmered together and strained. Chicken glaze, lemon juice and chopped chervil were blended in just before serving.

VÉNITIENNE

For eggs and poultry. Chopped chervil, parsley and shallots are cooked in vinegar before the incorporation of allemande sauce and spinach butter.

VILLEROI

This is used to coat foodstuffs before dipping them in egg and breadcrumbs for deep frying. Allemande sauce is mixed with both stock and mushroom *fumet* and reduced. When it is thick enough to coat a spoon, it should be left to cool before using.

TOMATO SAUCE

Usually tomato sauce is made from a foundation of concentrated tomato paste. This comes from a well established aesthetic principle that this sauce ought to have both the consistency and the appearance that we nowadays expect. These two conditions are difficult to achieve with fresh tomatoes, at any rate as regards the colour. For my part, I am inclined to prefer the second solution, that is, using fresh tomato *coulis* (thick tomato purée). I have however known some excellent sauce cooks who have been happy to use roux, tomato concentrate, light stock, seasoning and a bouquet garni. My father used to prepare a mixture of chopped garlic, shallots, garlic and pine kernels which he would cook very gently until translucent, in goose or pork fat. He would add a little flour, the tomato *coulis* (though this he

would sometimes replace by concentrate) and a bouquet garni. Then he added seasoning, moistened the whole with water and cooked the sauce for two or three hours in the oven.

Tomato sauce played an important part in the gastronomy of the south-west of France, because it was served, garnished with capers, as an accompaniment to *bouilli*, the special dish of boiled beef served on feast days.

All the evidence suggests that my father's method is best. It can be varied in different ways. Onions, garlic, shallots roughly chopped; the use of fresh tomatoes, cut up and left to dry, will necessitate straining, first through a tammy cloth and then through a conical sieve.

The dilution of an espagnole with tomato concentrate, reseasoned, preferably rather generously with pepper, is an equally good recipe.

One may be faced with having to improvise a tomato sauce. In this case a concentrate or paste, heated, strongly seasoned with cayenne pepper and salt, gives a fair imitation, especially if one has taken the trouble to add some thyme leaves and grated nutmeg. However, this method is not recommended as, although it may pass muster, one can never be sure of success.

The uses of tomato sauce are many and various, but it must be admitted that it is nowadays considered a minor, rather ordinary sauce.

It marries well with eggs, fish (especially as an accompaniment to fried fish), offal, boiled meat, pastas, roasts and vegetables. It is perhaps essentially a sauce of all trades. One can slightly modify the presentation by garnishing it with sliced pickled *cornichons*, baby cucumbers, or with *chanterelles*, or black or green olives. All that is very easy, and perhaps rather too much so, as the result of which the popularity of the sauce has conferred on it a certain degree of vulgarity. It has, in spite of this criticism, a very genuine vocation to certain dishes, among them tongue with tomato sauce and *chanterelles*, spaghetti, spare-ribs with tomato sauce and pickles, etc. *Sauce Orly*, served with fried fish, is a classical example of tomato sauce.

BREAST OF VEAL WITH PIMENTOS (*Tendrons de Veau aux Piments Forts*)
Illustrating the use of a tomato sauce.
6 servings:

6 lb. veal
10 oz. shallots
3 oz. garlic
3 lb. tomatoes
basil
6 hot pimentos
salt and pepper
2 oz. butter
2 oz. oil

Cut up a large *tendron* (breast) of veal so as to allow ¾ lb. to 1 lb. per person. Salt and pepper the meat all over. Flour and fry to take colour on both sides in a mixture of 2 oz. butter and 2 oz. oil. Dry the meat and reserve.

In the same casserole colour the 10 oz. shallots, finely chopped, and 3 oz. garlic peeled but in cloves. When it begins to turn golden add the tomatoes which have been peeled, cored, the seeds removed, and pulped; a big sprig of basil; the juice of the pulped tomatoes, and the hot pimentos cut open and cored. Leave the casserole for about $1\frac{1}{2}$ hours over a low fire. Serve just as it is.

SOME VARIATIONS OF TOMATO SAUCE

BULGARE
Tomato sauce with diced celery added to it.

BYRON
Italienne sauce with the addition of some claret wine and chopped truffles.

CZARDAS
Tomato sauce with paprika pepper and finished with cream.

FRANÇOIS
Tomato sauce to which should be added sliced mushrooms and flavoured with tarragon and butter.

SAUCE ORLY
Served with fried fish, this is a classical example of tomato sauce. To make this add tomato purée, meat extract and some butter to a suprême sauce.

ITALIENNE
Add chopped mushrooms, ham and some mixed herbs to a tomato sauce for this.

HOT EMULSIFIED SAUCES

The simplest of these sauces is *beurre blanc*. This is best prepared by lengthening the emulsion with buttermilk, vinegar and white wine. I do not mean to say that this is an emulsion such as milk, being a stable mixture of water and fat. Emulsified sauces are not only a mixture but a noble mixture. Starting from a liquid fatty substance, the sauce is changed and the mixture sometimes becomes a firm sauce. The texture of *beurre blanc* is due to chemical changes. Advances in food hygiene may one day make it difficult to make *beurre blanc* if fresh farmhouse butter is no longer made, whose hygienic imperfections are the very reason for its success in the sauce

To make *beurre blanc* successfully, first chop shallots and cover generously with vinegar and reduce the volume by cooking rapidly over a good heat. Strain, let it cool and add softened butter little by little, beating continuously. It is very difficult to make this sauce properly, because not only is a certain sleight of hand required, but certain conditions must be fulfilled.

At all events, *sabayon* can compensate for the difficulties of making *beurre blanc*. *Sabayon* is the French form of *zabaglione*, the Italian sweet, a kind of sauce of egg yolks blended and emulsified and steamed into a mousse. It is usually described as a sweet cream. I remember a cook from the Var who used to make *sabayon* by breaking one eggshell in half to separate the yolk and white and kept the half shell, which she used as a measure for the sugar and liqueur, so that the proportions of equal quantities of sugar, egg and liqueur, were maintained. This mixture was whisked in a *bain-marie* and became first frothy and then stiff. It must be taken off the heat and cooking stopped before it turns into a sort of scrambled egg mixture.

Nowadays, *zabaglione* or *sabayon* is sometimes served, pure and simple, by certain chefs who do the cooking actually at the customer's table. It is a debatable method and one much talked about.

The great majority of hot emulsified sauces are prepared in much the same way as *zabaglione*. Put the required number of egg yolks in a bowl. It is well known that it is very difficult to beat the yolks of two eggs, let alone a single one. But three or more are easy. In practice, three egg yolks will be enough for four or five people. Use half a pound of butter to every three eggs. Now add the same volume of water as eggs. Warm in a *bain-marie* or double saucepan, whisking the whole time. Never let the mixture get hotter than is bearable to the fingertips. Continue whisking until it is frothy. When the whisking brings the mixture away from the bottom of the pan, the sauce is cooked. This is the sign of perfection. Season discreetly with salt and cayenne pepper, clarify and let it cool. Add the juice of half a lemon and stand it in a warm spot. It is not necessary to strain or reheat this sauce, and it is the basis of all the others.

The stability of emulsions is maintained by electrical charges, but other factors play a part. Two ingredients help in this, shallots and paprika. The best results are achieved in conjunction with an acid, such as vinegar, lemon juice or white wine. The white wine, being much less acid than vinegar, must be reduced much more. During the reduction, add the pepper.

There are many recipes in existence, and many more can be invented. Nearly always, these start with a reduction of the vinegar with the addition of coarsely ground pepper. Some people salt lightly at the beginning, but I prefer to do this during the course of the preparation and correct it at the end. Shallots play a considerable role in the making of *Béarnaise* sauces and their derivatives.

How is reduction best accomplished? Obviously there is nothing to be gained by prolonging this over the fire. On the contrary, a rapid reduction implies constant supervision and the consequent rapid cooling of the pan.

This is done in the simplest possible manner in iced or cold water. When the reduction has reached the right moment, depending on the thickness of the pan, take it off the heat, but as this will not immediately stop the cooking and evaporation, cool it at once to prevent further reduction. Obviously, if you can judge in advance when the right moment is going to come and can withdraw the pan just before reduction is complete, so much the better. This calls for good timing and a lot of experience. The aim should always be to simplify procedure. For reasons difficult to explain, I prefer to add water to a reduction rather than to use it before evaporation of the liquid is completed. Among the hot emulsified sauces are *hollandaise*, *Béarnaise*, *Choron*, *Tyrolienne*, *mousquetaire*, *Mireille* and *aurore*.

SAUCE À LA HOLLANDAISE
Blanch some parsley and chop it very finely. Put in a saucepan with two large pats of fresh Vambre butter, a third pat rolled in flour, a little good stock, the juice of a lemon, salt, coarse pepper and a chopped anchovy. Blend this sauce on the fire, and serve with whatever dish you deem appropriate.

(La Nouvelle Cuisine, 1751)

SAUCE RÉMOULADE CHAUDE
Take some chives, shallots, mushrooms, capers and a little parsley and chop them all finely; do them separately for perfection. Put them in a saucepan with two or three spoonfuls of good quality oil. Put them on the fire, moisten with some purée (*coulis*), either thick or thin, and a little vinegar. When it has boiled, take off the fat and season well. Add some mustard. Warm the sauce but do not boil it, and you will have a tasty sauce.

(Traité Historique et Pratique de la Cuisine, 1758)

SAUCE HOLLANDAISE AU SUPRÊME
Break six eggs into a stewpan, add a little good quality butter, salt, finely-ground pepper, grated nutmeg, a tablespoonful of allemande sauce and a dessertspoonful of chicken glaze. Heat this sauce over a low fire, stirring well until it is blended; add a little butter three or four times, being careful to stir continually. Just before serving, pour in a little vinegar to make it tasty and a little lighter, and add a final good lump of butter.

(L'art de la cuisine française, Carême, 1835)

SAUCE HOLLANDAISE

Melt a piece of butter as big as an egg in a saucepan. Blend with half a dessertspoonful of stock, a little salt, grated nutmeg and coarsely ground pepper. Pour in boiling water and stir until the mixture becomes light and creamy. Add the yolks of 5 eggs one at a time, without ceasing to stir. When the sauce has become thick and smooth, add butter to it as you would for a mayonnaise. Strain. If it is too thick, add a few drops of water. Add lemon juice and serve.

(Le Bon Cuisinier, L. Souchay, 1886)

SAUCES FOR BURGUNDIAN FONDUE (*Sauces pour Fondue Bourguignonne*)

Illustrating the use of hot emulsified sauces.

6 servings:

6 yolks of eggs

6 tablespoonfuls water

16 fl. oz. (1 pint) olive oil (warmed)

6 tablespoonfuls vinegar

salt and pepper

1 tablespoonful mustard

1 tablespoonful tomato purée

1 tablespoonful anchovy purée

Put the yolks of eggs, water and vinegar into a thick-bottomed casserole. Beat over a low fire until the mixture is first frothy and then firm. Great attention must be paid because the eggs have to be heated enough to cook them but not so much that they begin to turn into scrambled eggs. Add salt and pepper and stir in the warmed olive oil a little at a time. Place the mustard, the tomato purée and the anchovy purée each in a separate receptacle and blend the sauce into them delicately and a little at a time. There is of course no reason to divide the sauce evenly into three. This is a matter of taste where one person may prefer to have more of one variety and less of another.

These sauces, which are destined for use with a *fondue Bourguignonne*, are also suitable accompaniments to a number of other preparations, particularly with vegetables such as asparagus, broccoli, broad beans, etc.

The *fondue Bourguignonne* itself is made up of a quantity of little cubes of meat cooked in very hot oil and kept hot at table on a heater of some sort. The guests pick up the meat with special long-handled forks and dip it into the sauce of their choice.

SOME VARIATIONS OF HOT EMULSIFIED SAUCES

BAVAROISE

For shellfish and fish. Wine vinegar, butter, horse-radish and shrimp butter, seasoned with salt, pepper and nutmeg are the constituents of this variation of a hot emulsified sauce.

BÉARNAISE

For grilled meats, more particularly associated with steak. This is one of the most famous of the hot emulsified sauces and is very popular with fillet of beef. The name is misleading as the sauce is not peculiar to Béarn, but was in fact named by the chef of the Pavillon Henri IV at St Germain-en-Laye, Paris, who introduced it in 1835. There are some variations of *Béarnaise* which have their own names, such as *Beauharnais*, a *Béarnaise* with tarragon butter and *Choron*, one with concentrated tomato paste or purée as an addition. *Béarnaise* is the classic mixture of fresh herbs, (tarragon, chervil, thyme and bay leaf), chopped and cooked with shallots in white wine. Yolks of eggs are whisked in a double saucepan, butter is added and the herb and wine mixture blended into the sauce.

HOLLANDAISE

For eggs, fish and vegetables. The classical mixture of butter and yolks of eggs cooked *au bain-marie* is seasoned with lemon juice and tarragon vinegar.

MALTAISE

For boiled vegetables. Add grated orange peel and juice from blood oranges to a hollandaise sauce. Or use tangerine peel and a few drops of curaçao. There is also a cold *sauce Maltaise* which is simply a mayonnaise with the same variations.

MOUSSELINE
For fish and boiled vegetables. Sometimes known as *Chantilly*, it is a hollandaise sauce with whipped cream added at the very last moment.

PALOISE
For grilled meat and poultry. A variant of *Béarnaise* in which mint is substituted for tarragon.

COLD EMULSIFIED SAUCES

The best example of these is mayonnaise. That it was invented at the siege of Fort Mahon seems doubtful to me, but this is unimportant. In the Middle Ages, *mayons* meant yolks of eggs, and the sauce made from these might well have been a mayonnaise.

The method of making mayonnaise is very well known. Yolks of eggs are mixed with oil, this is well seasoned and behold, there is your mayonnaise. The old method, by hand, was to begin with the egg yolks and seasoning, gradually adding the oil until the mixture thickened and solidified.

To be successful, there are a few precautions that must be taken:
1. Make sure that all the ingredients, above all the eggs and oil, are the same moderate temperature. Cold eggs and tepid oil will blend badly, as will cold oil and warm eggs
2. Do not try to make small quantities
3. Start with the egg yolks, mustard and vinegar all mixed together into a single fluid
4. If the mayonnaise becomes too thick, add some boiling vinegar either during the mixing, or at the end, to keep the emulsion stabilized.

For some years now, electric blenders have been manufactured which will make wonderful mayonnaises in a matter of seconds. These appliances make it possible to produce all kinds of variations, using the whole egg (indeed, even including the shell) and putting all the ingredients in at once before starting to blend. It would be absurd to make relatively small

quantities of mayonnaise by other means than using an electric blender. However, it is useful to know a method with which our children will probably not be familiar. I do not know if you have heard the story of the child who came in a state of amazement and showed his father a photograph of an old gramophone, saying how extraordinary it was that this machine did not need electricity and could be wound up with a handle. It will probably be considered equally bizarre to future generations that we could ever have made a mayonnaise with a metal egg whisk.

Nowadays the proportions of the ingredients are also completely reversed, modern processes allowing for very small quantities of yolk of egg or of whole egg in proportion to the volume of oil. That is to say, 2–3 yolks to every pint of oil.

Here are the quantities given by a very good restaurant as used today: 6–8 eggs to every 1¾ pints (2¼ pints) or litre of oil. Mustard, salt, cayenne pepper and vinegar. My own advice is to use 8 yolks of eggs, Dijon mustard equal in volume to the yolks, and the same of vinegar; the juice of a lemon, salt, cayenne pepper, and the same quantity of paprika. Mix all these together but do not beat. Pour in a coffeespoonful of oil (one-third olive oil to two-thirds groundnut oil). Let it be completely absorbed before repeating the operation. Do this several times. This is contrary to the usual practice of pouring the oil in a steady stream. When about 9 fl. oz. (just over 1 cup) have been absorbed, pour the rest of the oil, half or a third at a time, but still making sure that all the oil has been absorbed before adding a further quantity.

Any number of sauces can be made by this method and all are absolutely enchanting. The best known of these are *sauce tartare, sauce Tyrolienne, sauce verte, sauce Chantilly, mousquetaire, gribiche, sauce rémoulade, sauce Vincent,* and *sauce Suédoise.*

If an electric blender is used, you can make some very amusing sauces and use all kinds of unexpected ingredients, such as tomatoes, ketchup, Worcestershire sauce, *Nuoc-mam,* soya sauce, or seafish – anchovies, sardines, herrings, smoked salmon. Also smoked tongue, sweetbreads, brains, white chicken meat and all sorts of *pâtés.* Or maybe vegetables, sorrel, spinach, celery, fennel, paprika and sweet and hot peppers. Generous quantities of herbs such as chervil, parsley, chives or more discreet amounts of tarragon, garlic, cloves, shallots or onion. Composite or single spices, cooked white of egg which one does not generally know what to do with, meat and fish essences, all can be used. In fact, anything goes well with mayonnaise.

If I may enlarge, the very reliable reaction of mayonnaise-based sauces to heat has led to a wide variety of uses. More and more in modern cuisine the tendency has developed to use cold emulsified sauces as accompaniments to hot dishes. It has long been the practice to accompany a hot calf's head with a *sauce gribiche* or a poached fish with a *tartare,* but now the habit is spreading more and more to roasts and to vegetables. The use of these sauces is therefore subject to no recognizable bounds.

In the old days mayonnaise was the key to using up left-overs, of which *coquilles* of fish and cold meat salads were the *leit-motif*. If lobster mayonnaise and cold cuts are still served in this fashion one has nevertheless the chance of cooking lobster *à la corse* under the grill, and of serving a salad Marco Polo by garnishing avocado pears with crabmeat and covering them with mayonnaise . . . the possibilities are limitless.

SAULCE VERTE
Take bread, ginger, parsley; pound them well. Add verjuice and sharp wine.

(Le Viandier, Taillevent, c. 1390)

SAULCE VERT D'ESPICES
Pound ginger, cloves, *graine* and take out of the mortar. Then pound parsley, or *salemonde,* sorrel, marjoram, or two of these, the inside of a white loaf soaked in verjuice. Pour off the liquid and pound very well again. Put the spices, the herbs, the liquid all together and season with vinegar.

(Le Menagier de Paris, c. 1393)

SAUSSE VERTE
Take unripe corn and pound it in a mortar with a round of bread. Take out when pounded and strain through a cloth, season with pepper and salt and moisten with a little veal gravy and vinegar. When enough liquid has been added and it is well strained, serve it cold with lamb.

(Le Nouveau Cuisinier Royal et Bourgeois, Massialot, 1748)

SAUCE VERTE À L'OSEILLE
Take a handful of sorrel and pound it in a mortar; take care that the sorrel is dry or else the juice will be watery. When the sorrel is well pounded, strain off the juice through a tammy cloth. Put into the juice two pats of Vambre butter and a third which has been blended with a little flour. Season with salt and coarse pepper. Blend the sauce over the fire and serve with the appropriate dish, whether a rich or a simple one.

(La Nouvelle Cuisine, 1751)

SAUCE À LA RÉMOULADE
Chop very finely together parsley, chives, capers, anchovies and a little bit

of garlic; put everything in a pan with a spoonful of mustard, fine salt and
ground pepper. Stretch it all with oil and vinegar; taste the sauce so that
it is right, and nothing is too dominant. Serve in a sauceboat.

(Traité Historique et Pratique de la Cuisine, 1758)

SAUCE RÉMOULADE FROIDE

Put into a saucepan or some such kind of utensil the same ingredients as
we described for the hot *rémoulade* except for the mushrooms (*see* page 82).
Add one or two well-washed and chopped anchovies, season with salt and
coarse pepper. Dilute with a little mustard, oil and vinegar and beat everything well together. No one element should predominate. Serve cold. This
rémoulade will do with all kinds of cold roast chicken.

(Traité Historique et Pratique de la Cuisine, 1758)

SAUCE RÉMOULADE À LA RAVIGOTE

Blanch a handful of chervil mixed with a little tarragon, burnet, chives;
cool and strain and pound thoroughly with three hard-boiled yolks of eggs.
Add salt, pepper and grated nutmeg; then add a dessertspoonful of good
mustard, two tablespoonfuls of Aix oil and tarragon vinegar. Then strain
this purée through a cloth. The seasoning should be delicate and
appetizing.

(L'Art de la Cuisine française, Carême, 1835)

SAUCE RÉMOULADE À LA MOGUL

Pound four hard-boiled yolks of eggs in a mortar; add salt, pepper, grated
nutmeg and a pinch of cayenne pepper and paprika, a spoonful of caster
sugar, two large spoonfuls of oil and the same quantity of tarragon vinegar.
Pass the purée of this mixture through a cloth then add enough weak
saffron solution to give a good yellow colour and a dessertspoonful of very
finely-chopped chives. This sauce should have a strong taste, sufficient to
tickle the palate a little.

(L'Art de la Cuisine française, Carême, 1835)

SAUCE RÉMOULADE

Make some mayonnaise. Cut up very small 1 oz. of capers and 4 gherkins;
compress them and cut up again. First add a little tarragon and chopped
chervil; mix this with the capers and gherkins, and then thoroughly mix

with the mayonnaise. Secondly, mix in half a dessertspoonful of mustard and a pinch of cayenne pepper. Thoroughly mix the whole and serve.

(*Le Bon Cuisinier*, L. Souchay, 1886)

SAUCE VERTE

Chop 2 shallots, a quarter of a bay leaf, 2 chive roots, 2 sprigs of thyme and 4 of chervil. Put all these in a pan and stretch with 2 glasses of white wine and a dessertspoonful of vinegar. Reduce this completely until almost all the liquid is evaporated. Then add 1 tablespoonful of hollandaise sauce, a little cayenne pepper and some spinach water. Strain and serve.

(*Le Bon Cuisinier*, L. Souchay, 1886)

NEWFOUNDLAND POTATO SALAD (*Salade de Pommes de Terre Terre-Neuve*)

Illustrating the use of a cold emulsified sauce.

6 servings:

salad:
- **1 lb. new potatoes**
- **1 lb. cod fillets**
- **6 hard-boiled eggs**

sauce:
- **2 egg yolks**
- **1 tablespoonful Dijon mustard**
- **1 tablespoonful English mustard**
- **1 teaspoonful paprika**
- **6 anchovy fillets**
- **¼ teaspoonful cayenne**
- **½ teaspoonful salt**
- **¼ teaspoonful mono-sodium glutamate**
- **2 hard-boiled egg whites**
- **2 oz. chives**
- **4 dessertspoonfuls vinegar**
- **¼ pint (⅓ pint) olive oil**
- **½ pint (1¼ cups) corn oil**

In some suitable receptacle place the sauce ingredients. Blend with an electric beater or in a blender. Cut into slices 1 lb. new potatoes boiled in their skins and allowed to grow cold. Place them in a large porcelain bowl and add, well crumbled, 1 lb. cold boiled cod fillets.

Pour the sauce over this, stir it in and decorate with 6 hard-boiled eggs cut in half. As further decoration use a basis of herbs, tomatoes or pimentos.

ARTICHOKE HEARTS ANDRÉ ROSSIGNOL (*Fonds d'Artichauts André Rossignol*)

Illustrating the use of a tepid emulsified sauce.

6 servings:

6 large artichoke hearts
lemon juice
sauce:
10 oz. sorrel
3 egg yolks
3 dessertspoonfuls water
6 fl. oz. ($\frac{3}{4}$ cup) olive oil
salt, pepper

Prepare 6 large hearts of artichoke and cook them in boiling water lightly flavoured with lemon juice.

In a little casserole simmer the sorrel previously cleaned and dried in a cloth. When the sorrel is cooked, put it in a bowl and pulverize it with an electric beater.

Into a thick-bottomed casserole place the yolks of 3 eggs with 3 dessertspoonfuls of water and the pulverized sorrel. Warm the casserole over a slow fire, beating the yolks almost until they become frothy and cook them just sufficiently to ensure that they will give a respectable consistency to the sauce. Next add the olive oil, barely warm. Salt and pepper lightly. Place the artichoke hearts on a serving dish and pour the sauce over them. *Serve tepid.*

It should be noted that artichoke hearts may be cooked in the classic manner in what is commonly known as *à blanc*. This preparation is made as follows: bring 2 pints ($2\frac{1}{2}$ pints) of lightly-salted water to the boil. In a bowl beat together 3 tablespoonfuls flour with 6 of vinegar and 6 of water. Pour the resulting mixture into the boiling water while beating vigorously. One can then cook the artichoke by adding a piece of fat from a beef kidney. This fat serves to coat the surface of the liquid and enables one to cook without a lid but to avoid spilling over like boiling milk.

It must be admitted that artichoke hearts cooked in this bouillon are less elegant in appearance, but rather better in flavour.

SOME VARIATIONS OF COLD EMULSIFIED SAUCES

AÏOLI
Especially associated with *Brandade de Morue* (*see* page 76) it is delicious with eggs and chicken dishes. It is a very thick mayonnaise heavily flavoured with pounded garlic. Lemon juice is used, not vinegar.

ANCHOVY
For cold fish, hors d'oeuvre. Anchovy paste is pounded with hard-boiled yolks of eggs; oil and vinegar are incorporated and seasoning to taste.

COLLIOURE
For cold fish, hors d'oeuvre and salads. Mayonnaise with anchovy paste, grated garlic and chopped parsley.

CRESSONNIÈRE
Hard-boiled yolks of eggs and chopped watercress with oil, vinegar and purée of anchovies.

DIJONNAISE
For fish, hors d'oeuvre and salads. Dijon mustard is pounded or mashed with hard-boiled yolks of eggs, salt and pepper. Oil and lemon juice are blended in the usual way.

GRIBICHE
For cold fish and shellfish. Chopped gherkins and capers are folded into a sauce made from pounded hard-boiled yolks of eggs, seasoning, which has been blended with oil and vinegar. Whites of eggs cut in strips are folded in before serving.

INDIENNE
For eggs, chicken, meat and vegetables. A mayonnaise seasoned with curry and chopped chives.

MALTAISE
For asparagus. Mayonnaise with the addition of the juice of a blood orange and strips of finely cut orange peel.

MOUSQUETAIRE
For eggs, hors d'oeuvre, cold meat and salads. Again a variation of mayonnaise. Chopped shallots cooked in white wine are mixed with meat glaze and blended into the mayonnaise. The seasoning is heightened with cayenne pepper.

NIÇOISE
For salads. Chopped sweet peppers, tomato purée and chopped tarragon leaves are sieved and added to a mayonnaise.

PARISIENNE
For cold asparagus. *Petit Suisse* or Philadelphia cream cheese is pounded and seasoned with salt and paprika. Oil and vinegar are added as for mayonnaise and chopped chervil is added as a final touch.

SARDALAISE
Hard-boiled yolks of eggs are mashed with thick cream. Add sieved truffles, blend oil and lemon juice as for mayonnaise and a little Armagnac.

SUÉDOISE
For roast goose and cold pork. A mayonnaise which is blended with unsweetened apple sauce, mustard and grated horse-radish.

VERTE
This may be a mayonnaise with the addition of parsley, chives and tarragon minced finely together with a little water. Chopped chives or onion juice may be added to the mixture. Alternatively, it may be a mayonnaise, blended with aspic jelly and a purée of herbs which is used as a coating. If chopped hard-boiled yolks and whites of eggs are added, *sauce verte* becomes *sauce Vincent*.

SECONDARY SAUCES
AND CONSIDERATIONS
ON FLAVOURING

BITTER-SWEET SAUCES

The basic element in these sauces is either veal stock or an espagnole. The addition of a mixture of caramelized sugar or honey and vinegar confers on them a very characteristic appearance and distinction.

The most frequent use of these sauces is with *canard à l'orange* and going on from there to duck with various fruits, peaches, apricots, cherries, lychees and so forth.

I have also used them quite successfully to accompany veal (especially *tendron*) as well as guinea-fowl, geese, turkeys, pheasants and shellfish.

In Roman cookery (of the classical period) and in oriental cookery, these sauces are even more frequently used. This field is wide open to the audacious but it would be a pity to serve ortolans with this sauce.

SAUCE BORDELAISE

Sauce Bordelaise, along with *marchand de vin*, *Bercy*, *maître de chai*, is essentially a sauce made on the instant. At one time it made use either of veal stock or meat glaze. It is obvious that these sauces are suitable for more uses than their traditional appearance with grills. There is no reason to prevent one's imagination from straying in the direction of fish, chicken or game. Possible examples are: roast hare, *sauce marchand de vin;* angler fish, *sauce Bordelaise;* partridge, *sauce Bercy;* pheasant, *sauce maître de chai.*

One should beware of unnecessary fears on the part of one's imagination, especially when they serve no purpose.

According to the classical tradition, a *Bordelaise* sauce should be based on white wine. The same sauce made with red wine should, strictly speaking, be called *marchand de vin*. For some time, however, *sauce Bordelaise* has been more and more linked with red wine. It is, therefore, not unacceptable today to prepare it with a Médoc or St Emilion.

SAUCE BORDELAISE

4 servings:
½ bottle red wine
4 large shallots
**4 tablespoonfuls veal
  stock**
½ clove garlic
beurre manié :
⅔ oz. flour
1 oz. butter

If one intends to use this sauce to accompany an entrecôte, one should cook the entrecôte in a shallow *sautoir* and, when the meat is nearly ready, set it aside in a second pan in which it can very gently finish its cooking. Drain off the fat from the first pan and add to it the shallots, garlic and the red wine. Reduce by two-thirds. Next add the veal stock and bring quickly to the boil. Season with salt and pepper. Bind with the *beurre manié*, pour over the entrecôte and serve at once.

It is possible, as an alternative method, to start the preparation by lightly colouring the shallots and garlic, in which case a little butter must be added to the list of ingredients. Using this method, one should deglaze the *sautoir* before adding the shallots and garlic. This operation is carried out with the wine set aside for the sauce as soon as the shallots have coloured sufficiently. The use of garlic is not strictly classical and moderation must be the watchword. It should be cooked to a perfect golden shade. A sauce of this type is dark and the right colour before beginning the liaison, which must be progressive and will be flavoured by the presence of the cooked butter in the sauce. The *beurre manié* should therefore be added a little at a time.

CHAUD-FROID SAUCES

It is clear that there are two types of these cold sauces, white (cream base) and brown (game base). One can apply either to almost anything, be it eggs, fish, shellfish, offal, poultry, butcher's meat, game or vegetables.

The *chaud-froid* sauce is to a large extent capable of the same functions as a cold emulsified sauce.

For obscure symbolic reasons one tends to match the colour of the sauce to the colour of the dish which it is to accompany, with the exception that certain white foods (sweetbreads, *fricandeau*, white fish, white vegetables) are tolerated with brown sauces. On the other hand, there exists a sort of repugnance to using white sauces with red meat, a repugnance which has no gastronomic justification.

Cold game sauces are likewise traditionally brown, a tradition which I also decline to accept as gospel.

The function of a *chaud-froid* may also be decorative. White *chaud-froid* is discussed in relation to velouté sauces (*see* page 71) and the brown variety under espagnole sauces (*see* page 53).

FISH AND SHELL-FISH SAUCES

Other than fish velouté, fish sauces have little place in the concept of the cuisine of today. If one aims to make a salmon *à la Chambord* it is not likely that the accompanying sauce will be mentioned on the menu.

In the modern kitchen, sauces are assuming more and more specific functions, and a fish sauce (velouté) has few outlets beyond the requirements of banquets and weddings. It is true, however, that this sauce can be delicious and is by no means fragile. Enriched by the addition of seafood and mushrooms it will appear as *Dieppoise, Normande, Cancaloise, Quimperloise*, etc.

Fish sauces today are made at a moment's notice and are adapted to the fish which they are destined to accompany. Their base is a simple fish stock and the liaison is made by the addition of hollandaise sauce.

Sauce Américaine, which is the basis for all shellfish sauces, is the only fish sauce with multiple uses. In the cuisine of the present day (and I must repeat this) most sauces-of-all-work have had their day.

The cost to the client of a high quality *sauce Américaine* has greatly restricted its use beyond shell-fish themselves. Angler fish *à l'Américaine* prepared on its own base would be a mediocre preparation; the same dish making use of a lobster sauce simply would not be justifiable.

In fact only two essential uses remain: in a *bisque*, which is a soup, and in variants of *sauce Nantua*.

The thread of *sauce Américaine* decorating a fish dish can well be replaced by a more generous use of a tomato sauce, a fact which has not escaped those professionals who decline to sacrifice everything to decoration.

There are few lobster sauces; rather, there are variations on the main theme. All fish, without exception can be accompanied by it and its derivatives are numerous. One should begin by mentioning *beurre d'écrevisses* or *beurre de homard*, shrimp or lobster butter, which have had their hour of glory and have gradually disappeared. The method has never appealed to me. To make these sauces one pulverizes all the shells and contents (after the extraction of the meat) as finely as possible with a mortar and pestle and one cooks them very gently and for a very long time in butter. One can make use of these by clarifying them and adding them as reinforcement to sauces such as *Nantua*, that is to say basically to a béchamel, a *Mornay* or a velouté.

Bisques and *coulis* can be prepared by more than one method but these are not important as long as the final result is excellent.

One important characteristic of crustaceans is that they can be used with a much wider variety of sauces than they can, basically, provide themselves. Classic sauces such as thermidor, Newburg and mayonnaise benefit by purely external additions of shellfish. This is obvious when one realizes that only the noblest shellfish give really good results in sauce. I use lobster exclusively for the base of a *sauce Américaine*. Dublin Bay prawns, crabs, and even crayfish give mediocre results. Apart from a prawn *coulis* the only serious shellfish sauce seems to me to be the *Américaine*. For the record I will set down the recipe for crayfish in Banyuls wine (*civet de langouste au vin de Banyuls*). The same dish may be prepared with red wine, but in either case it goes without saying that lobster is even better!

Choose a female, without eggs if possible. The eggs of the lobster have no gastronomic properties but are very colourful and decorative. Even that cannot be said of the crayfish. Females are to be recognized by the eggsack beneath the tail. In the male this is undeveloped; in the female, it is much longer and covered with a skin and criss-crossed.

Cut the crayfish tail into sections and the body in half. Extract the coral and blend it with butter. Reduce. Remember to throw out the little 'pebbles' at the very end of the shell. Sauté the crayfish very briskly in a mixture of two-thirds oil and one-third butter, then take it out and dry it. In the same casserole cook a fine *mirepoix* of carrots, shallots, celery, onion

and garlic. When the mixture has taken colour replace the crayfish and moisten very liberally with Banyuls wine. Add a large bouquet garni. Let it cook for not more than 15 minutes. Add to the mixture of coral and butter a little flour and a dash of Cognac. Bind the sauce with this mixture by adding the sauce little by little to the binding element until there is enough liaison to allow you to reverse the process by adding the increased liaison back gradually into the sauce. If the Banyuls is replaced by a red wine it is advisable to add a little sugar. One can also flame the finished dish but although this method is very popular in south-west France it does not seem to me necessary. (One can relate the use of *sauce Américaine* to a recipe for chicken Nantua.)

Aïoli with Mackerel (*Aïoli aux Maquereaux*)

CHICKEN STUFFED WITH LOBSTER (*Poulet au Homard*)

Illustrating the use of a lobster sauce.

6 servings:

This recipe is inspired by chicken Nantua and preparations of the same sort with a prawn sauce. If I have deserted prawns it is because they are less good than in my young days. It is still possible to find excellent ones, but even so the sauces to be derived from them are less elegant than those based on lobster.

1 superb 6 lb. chicken

1 small live lobster (preferably female, *see* **page 99)**

1½ pints (2 pints) concentrated chicken velouté

6 yolks of eggs

1 pint (1¼ pints) thick cream

1 pint (1¼ pints) chicken mousseline

1 tablespoonful butter

1 tablespoonful oil

1 wineglassful Armagnac or Cognac

bunch of tarragon

4 dessertspoonfuls chopped shallots

2 medium-sized cloves of garlic

½ pint (1¼ cups) very good dry white wine

1 lb. tomatoes

2 celery hearts

salt, pepper, cayenne pepper

Cook the lobster *à l'américaine*. Since the lobster is small, cut it in two lengthways. Remove the pouch and throw it out. Set aside the coral, which should be abundant in a female. This coral is the creamy-coloured substance lodged inside the shell. In shade it ranges from pale green to chestnut in an uncooked lobster and takes on a delicate shade of pink after cooking. These colours possess a rare quality which it is impossible to counterfeit. If the female is carrying eggs these too should be extracted and reserved. (Once the eggs have been crushed either with a spatula or the back of a spoon they will serve to colour any fish sauce you like, but particularly the one which we are now discussing. To obtain satisfactory results, however, the eggs *must* be crushed, but carefully, or by the application of too much pressure they may turn red and cease to be of use. It is only for their colour that one needs them. From the point of view of sauce and sauce only, however, an eggless female is much to be preferred for flavour.)

To proceed, put the butter and oil into a shallow casserole. Heat quickly. Add the halves of lobster and press the flesh

Chicken stuffed with Lobster (*Poulet au Homard*)

against the bottom of the casserole. Let it colour quickly before taking it out. Fire it in young Armagnac or Cognac, reserve and keep warm.

Add to the same casserole the chopped shallots and garlic. Let them cook for a little and then add the wine. Add a good sprig of tarragon. Add salt and cayenne pepper. Next add 1 lb. tomatoes, peeled, cored and crushed and cook the lot for 15 minutes. Withdraw the casserole and allow it to grow cold. Dry the lobster, remove the flesh from the shell, taking good care in the meantime not to waste any of the liquid. The lobster itself must be dry and clean at this stage.

Next place the lobster shell in a mortar and pound it thoroughly with a pestle. Pass through a *chinois* with the help of a little fish stock. If difficulty is experienced with this operation it can be omitted.

Blend the coral with the cream by beating energetically, or if necessary by mashing it in a bowl or a plate with a fork. This stage is of the greatest importance because if the coral is not thoroughly mixed and blended it is apt to lose a great deal of its quality.

Replace the casserole on the fire, bring to the boil and cook for a few minutes before adding the blended cream and coral. As a substitute for this blend one can, if necessary, use a béchamel or velouté in equivalent quantities. Bring the sauce to the boil while whipping it constantly. As soon as it boils, strain through a very fine sieve and then a muslin cloth. Butter the sauce (*see* page 22) and set it aside in a hot place, but not so hot that there is any risk of it boiling. It is always best at this juncture to use a fireproof glass or porcelain vessel.

Preparation of the chicken

Set aside the skin of the bird's neck. Bone the breast and remove the wishbone and rib cage. Leave intact the bones of the wings and legs, and the bird's spine. Salt and pepper the bird inside. Cut up the flesh of the lobster into small dice and mix them into the *mousseline* of chicken. Add 1 or 2 tablespoonfuls of cream if required and some truffle juice if you have any available. Stuff the bird with this mixture. Tie up the bird or sew it together using the skin of the neck and restore it as far as possible to its original shape.

Brown the bird in 5 oz. of clarified butter in a large casserole. When ready add 2 well-cleaned raw hearts of celery. Put the top on the casserole and leave for something under 1 hour over a very low flame. At the end of this time clarify the butter again because the water drawn from the celery hearts must be completely evaporated.

Withdraw the fowl and take out the stitches. Put it aside in a large well-warmed china *cocotte* and keep hot. Remove the celery hearts which you can now set aside for some other purpose (they would be delicious au gratin). Drain the casserole of all the butter used in the cooking, which can also be saved for some other purpose. Pour in a glass of port and loosen the extracts in the bottom of the pan which will have become a glaze of as much as a quarter of a pint. When this is done, add the lobster sauce. Mix well and keep stirring until it boils. The sauce must be neither thick nor runny, but smooth and creamy. Pour it over the chicken, bring up almost to boiling point and maintain at this temperature for about 30 minutes.

Truffles may be added, but discreetly. I prefer to use the liquid from truffles, as being less flamboyant.

Remember that in using lobster eggs in this or any other recipe, they must not be over-cooked after being pounded or mixed with a little cream. Add enough sauce to blend with the eggs, but this must always be tepid, before adding the rest of the sauce and then boiling it.

GAME SAUCES

In this field, even more than others, there is no universal 'game sauce'. A *civet*, a *poivrade*, a *Romaine*, a *Grand Veneur*, or a Cumberland sauce are prepared with a precise destination in mind.

In fact one can divide game sauces into two categories. First, those which are destined for small game (hares, pheasants, partridges, etc.) and which in general come under the headings of *civet*, *salmis*, *saupiquet* and so on. Second, the sauces for venison, wild boar, bear, etc. These are of the *poivrade* or *Grand Veneur* type and have many variants but on a common base. Their destination is perforce linked to the material which the chef knows is going to be available. I cannot imagine a cook nowadays stocking a quantity of Cumberland sauce unless he had a large quantity of venison or something similar in his reserves.

Leg of lamb or mutton *en chevreuil* is a vanished fashion because the gastronome of today, being unaccustomed to the dish, tends to suspect simply that the meat is high.

GARLIC

The use of garlic can give widely differing results according to its provenance and its freshness. I give elsewhere (*see* page 108) a very detailed recipe of a chicken cooked with garlic, which is the perfect demonstration of the possibilities offered by this condiment. Since the dawn of history in the Mediterranean basin, it has always been thought of as a sort of panacea. First the Egyptians, then the Greeks and the Romans, made great use of it until, little by little, as in our day, they began to consider that its aroma was vulgar. This almost always applied, however, to the raw state because, when it is cooked, whilst it retains its characteristic flavour, it becomes much less pungent.

In the past a number of cooks added garlic in small quantities to certain of their sauces in order to modify and improve the final result. It has always been very well suited to lobster *à l'américaine*, for instance. Another example is the favourable way in which certain sauces adapted themselves to the traces of garlic left by rubbing casseroles and earthenware dishes generally before using them. Originally this practice had nothing to do with flavouring since garlic was rubbed round the inside of a dish to protect its varnished surface. Later the practice was continued of rubbing garlic round dishes destined to contain, for instance, *gratin Dauphinois*, long after these were made of fireproof porcelain or glass. Garlic, just as vanilla, may be used in *bouillabaisse*, but with great discretion.

Fresh garlic is in fact more easily digested and less violent than old garlic. From the moment when the first green shoot appears on the knob it should be thrown away and not used. Another way to moderate its effect is to crush the garlic between two pieces of fine cloth or muslin. The oil containing the acid elements is then soaked up by the material and the use of garlic is considerably improved without actual loss of flavour.

The discreet use of garlic is nonetheless very useful in basic stocks which accept it. It goes without saying that espagnole sauce, fish stocks, anything with tomato, veal stocks and most ragoûts have everything to gain by it. As in all art, excess is deplorable.

Aïoli is a sauce which can be marvellous if handled intelligently. In the old days it was virtually a garlic purée 'mounted' on olive oil. This blend was delicate and for more than a century yolks of eggs have been added, a method which is satisfactory to all.

CHICKEN WITH GARLIC (*Poulet à l'Ail*)

4 servings:

3 lb. chicken
5 oz. garlic, peeled and chopped
1 pint (1¼ pints) dry white wine
1 tin unsweetened condensed milk
2 oz. (¼ cup) butter
2 fl. oz. (¼ cup) oil
salt and pepper

Divide the chicken into 8 pieces. Salt and pepper them and colour them in a *cocotte*. Withdraw them from the dish and replace them with the chopped garlic; stir this with a wooden spoon and cook to within an inch of its life. This point is only reached when the garlic begins to stick to the spoon. By then it will have progressed from a pale shade to a light brown colour. The wine should be added just at this moment and, in order not to waste a second, remember to have the bottle right by your hand. The success or failure of the operation will depend on the skill with which you add the wine at the critical moment.

When the wine has been added, replace the pieces of chicken in the *cocotte*, add salt (no pepper) and cook for 45 minutes.

Withdraw and place on the serving dish. Set the sauce over a hot flame and pour into it the condensed milk, bringing the whole mixture to a rolling boil. Pass it through a fine sieve over the chicken.

If this operation is carried out accurately, it is not possible to detect the garlic. This recipe, very much my own, will not benefit from being varied. I have experimented with everything ranging from herbs to Cognac without improving it. Attention to technique is therefore even more important than attention to quantities. The quantity of garlic is of course very important, and although it may seem excessive is actually nothing of the kind.

To sum up, garlic, when used with perception, can offer a great variety of undeniably interesting experiences. One must, however, remember that there is no comparison between garlic cooked among other vegetables and raw garlic such as one employs with snails or salads.

Finally, never forget that fresh parsley eaten *after* a quantity of garlic will remove almost all its traditional disadvantages. Roasted coffee grains chewed will serve the same purpose, but only for a short time.

HERBS

As with garlic, so there are certain herbs which are worth discussing. I have often had occasion to point out how the indiscreet use of tarragon can adversely affect the success of a sauce. It very quickly adds a bitter flavour. For this reason, when a sauce demands great care and delicacy of touch and flavour one should use only the freshest and tenderest tarragon leaves. The correct use of tarragon is therefore much more closely allied to that of truffles (*see* page 115) than of garlic. The same applies to basil which is very little used in French sauces. It is used in moderation in Provence but in great quantities in Niçois and Italian cooking. It is amusing to note that basil has become synonymous with *pistou*. If one ever asks the Niçois or Provençaux the meaning of *pistou*, they will imply that it is basil. This is quite incorrect, for the *pistou* is the mortar in which the oil, peppers and basil are blended together.

In all sauces, even the simplest, herbs are acceptable. There is nothing wrong, for instance, in cooking the milk for a béchamel with thyme, a bay leaf, basil or tarragon. Moderation and discretion, however, play an ineluctable part in sauces.

JUICES FROM ROAST MEAT

Juice from a roast of any kind does not qualify as a sauce in the current meaning of the term. It can however, and very happily, serve as a base in the practical construction of a sauce.

What is this juice? Either the liquid drained from a joint during roasting, or the same liquid first glazed and then liquefied afresh.

There are two schools of thought in roasting:

1. Without liquid. This is based on the theory of searing the outer surfaces of the meat in order to retain the natural juices within the roast. This method applies as much to red meat, which seems particularly adaptable to this method, as to white. In this case, one does not baste the roast during its cooking.

2. With the addition of liquid. This method applies to various roasts of pork, fat poultry and veal. At the beginning of the dish one adds to the roast a certain quantity of vegetables the function of which is to moisten the meat, and one adds to this both fat and water. During the process of roasting one also bastes it.

In both cases an additional *déglaçage* (*see* page 25) is always permissable. In the case of the first method it is preferable to remove the fat brought out by cooking and to de-glaze by means of wine or water (often water is to be preferred). In the old days, one used mostly to perform this operation with a clear stock or a bouillon, but the resulting gravy was not at all memorable and was unattractive in appearance. As far as colour goes, one can repair the damage with a tasteless meat essence or with commercial additives sold for the purpose.

In method 2 one dilutes the juices from the roast because of a tendency to excessive fat. In method 1, the fat is thrown out; in method 2, it is carefully preserved so that the *déglaçage* may be added to it.

One can still find sauceboats with two beaks, the purpose of which is to separate the fat from the juice of a gravy. Too much fat is to be avoided. If one wishes to bind and blend a gravy so that it is converted to a true sauce, then the fat *must* be removed. It must in fact be removed almost entirely because fat makes any blending very liable to separate. The binding elements should be potato flour well mixed with Madeira. In passing let it be pointed out that veal stock can (at a pinch) *always* be replaced by properly bound gravy from a roast. At the same time, this substitution is basically a second best and one should not fall into the habit of making it. An important detail here is the admirable way in which these gravies can be kept in modern refrigerators. One can in any household maintain so to speak, a modest emergency reserve. The fat extracted from a roast may be used for various purposes and is particularly good for frying potatoes.

YOUNG GUINEA FOWLS (*Pintadeaux Château Guiraud*)
Illustrating the use of juices of roasts

4 servings:

2 young guinea fowls
1 bottle Château Guiraud
1⅔ (2¼ pints) chicken stock
bouquet garni
onions
garlic
shallots
carrots
turnips
celery
fennel
30 Spanish olives
butter
½ pint (1¼ cups) cream
salt, pepper
cayenne pepper
paprika

Brown the vegetables and the heads, feet and giblets of the guinea fowls in butter; remove the fat, add the wine and enough stock to cover completely the birds.

When this comes to the boil remove the fat from the stock, correct the seasoning, cover and cook in a fairly hot oven. When the birds are ready, place them in a bowl. Strain the liquid and pour it over them. Leave till cold.

Next day, take out the guinea fowl. Lift off the layer of fat which will have formed. Remove the jellied stock and put this in a pan. Remove the thick deposit in the bottom of the bowl. Clarify this in the usual manner (*see* page 23).

Reserve one bird and bone the legs. Carve all the meat off the other one. Slice the finest cuts finely and put aside.

Pound the meat and the liver lightly cooked and creamed with butter. Work in the concentrates previously put aside. Add more butter till the mixture is the consistency of foie gras. Season well.

Set the carcass breast down so that it looks like a boat and fill with half the purée. Garnish with slices of the meat cut into fine strips, and slices spread with the remainder of the purée. Place the jelly and the olives, stoned blanched round the dish. Serve cold.

Serve an accompanying sauce made from the rest of the concentrated deposit from the bottom of the bowl which has been mixed with whipped cream and seasoned with paprika and cayenne pepper.

MUSHROOMS

There are two kinds of mushrooms, those from the woods and those from the fields. Among the wood mushrooms, *cêpes* (*boletus edulis*) are rarely used in sauces or their garnishes. *Morilles* (*morchella esculenta*), *girolle* or *chanterelle* (*cantharellus cibarius*), are on the contrary used too often. Horse mushrooms (*Agaricus arventis*) and field mushrooms (*Agaricus campestris*) are becoming rare and rarer. Cultivated mushrooms have been developed from hybrids of *A.campestris*. Cultivated mushrooms, such as the *champignon de Paris* or button mushroom, are too easily adapted to 'any old sauce'. It is worth noting here the complete disappearance from sauces and stocks of the peelings and odds and ends of mushrooms. Only occasionally is real mushroom stock still to be found. This might denote a decline in the quality of the material or a change of fashion. In fact, I suspect that it is due to the great development of mushroom cultivation that has changed our habits. Nowadays cultivated mushrooms are delivered absolutely fresh each day and we no longer peel them. They are cleaned, washed and used. I also suspect that the mushroom peelings which ended their career in the stockpot were put in more for economy than for any better reason.

The same reflection occurs to me on the subject of mushroom stock, for one must recognize the fact that a certain number of mushrooms are needed by the cook as garnishes or for decoration. The mushrooms, properly cleaned and prepared, are cooked in the following manner.

Put a little water in the bottom of a casserole and add to it the juice of a lemon, an ounce or two of butter and a good pinch of salt. Bring to the boil. Add the mushrooms. Replace the lid and cook for about four minutes. Only a little liquid is needed, the mushrooms containing enough themselves to provide the quantity required. It is this distillation of mushroom, the uses of which are rather limited, which one adds to sauces. I am not myself particularly enamoured of it although from time to time I make use of it.

Mushrooms which are to be used in a sauce should, in my opinion, be gently fried before use and, in order to give their best, in as quickly as possible. There is a theory that, in order to show off their qualities at their best, mushrooms should be enabled to re-absorb the vegetable liquid lost in this process. In fact the process is a little different. The natural liquid does indeed evaporate but perhaps it is better left in the mushroom. Undoubtedly the general practice of today with wood mushrooms such as *chanterelles* and *girolles* is to throw out the water which is drawn out of them by cooking, and then to cook them afresh, so to speak, dehydrated. It is only necessary to throw them into boiling water and they will lose their own liquid instantly. Afterwards, they should be dried in a colander or in linen. Some schools of thought prefer to use them in sauces after rissoling, (*see* page 31), some to use them raw. I have a personal prejudice for a method of my own.

Whatever type of mushroom I deal with, I prefer to cook without a lid, otherwise following the method outlined above. Butter, lemon juice, a little water, a little salt. I throw in the mushrooms and wait for the complete evaporation of the water, at which moment I throw in more butter and finish the operation over a brisk heat, seasoning suitably as I go. I would use this method at all times.

Let us take for instance a chicken cooked with morels (*morilles*) and a cream sauce. I should cut it up, sauté it in butter, season it, and set it to cook in a covered casserole for 20 minutes. During this time I should prepare the morels in a separate pan, adding cream and seasonings, leaving them to simmer for a few minutes and then adding the sauce to the chicken and continuing to simmer the whole over a very low fire for 20 minutes more. Since mushrooms have an extremely delicate perfume it is preferable not to mask this with strong flavours such as tarragon, basil, bay leaf or rosemary.

Mushrooms have played a great part recently in a kind of neo-gastronomic folklore; in the form of *duxelles* (*see* page 172) one was apt to stumble on them at any stage of the proceedings in '*hostelleries gastronomiques*'. The traditional mushroom sauce which used in my young days to accompany the Sunday fillet of beef was savoury enough, but today's version is nonetheless distinctly better.

CHICKEN FLAMBÉ (*Poulet Flambé*)

Illustrating the use of cream and mushrooms in sauces.

6 servings:

a prime chicken of 4 lb.	In a wide, deep *cocotte*, lightly brown the
10 oz. mushrooms	chicken, having cut it into 12 pieces.
3 oz. (over ¼ cup) butter	Salt and add a touch of pepper. When
3 fl. oz. (over ¼ cup) oil	it is well browned add the mushrooms
3 fl. oz. (over ¼ cup) Cognac	and sauté them as well. Warm the Cognac, set fire to it and pour it over the
a large sprig of tarragon	chicken. Add the sprig of tarragon. Put
12 fl. oz. (1½ cups) thick cream	the lid on the *cocotte* and cook on a very low flame for 45 minutes.
pinch potato flour	Take out the chicken and the mush-
3 dessertspoonfuls port wine	rooms and let them dry off on the serving dish (with the aid of a skimmer). Drain

three-quarters of the fat from the *cocotte*, along with the tarragon. Replace the *cocotte* over maximum heat, add the cream and beat till it comes to a rolling boil. Move to the edge of the burner.

Carefully stir the port wine into the potato flour and when perfectly smooth add the mixture to the sauce, bring it to the boil and pour at once over the chicken. Serve with rice *à la chinoise* or creole rice.

TRUFFLES

This 'diamond in a kitchen's coronet' contributes effectively to the nobility of sauces. Nevertheless, the mere presence of truffles in a sauce does not automatically guarantee exceptional quality.

First, one must discriminate between one truffle and another. There are truffles from Périgord, from Vaucluse, from Spain and Italy. There are truffle years, vintage years so to speak, and there are years when hardly any truffles grow. There are seasons when the truffles are attacked by worms, just as olives sometimes are, and there are others when they are not only excellent but also abundant. It is rather odd that, in general, abundance and quality coincide.

The truffle is a mushroom and not, as used to be thought, some happy freak of nature. Fresh, raw truffles are the best; preserved truffles vary widely according to the method of conservation employed. In the old days they used to be preserved under a coat of fat, in oil or in preparations of salt. Today they are vacuum packed, or placed raw in sealed tins, and give excellent results.

In practice there is no reason why truffles should not be used as garnishing for sauces. Whatever the sauce, be it as widely different as fish stock from béchamel, the end result will be ennobled by the addition of truffles. It is important to allow them the important role they play by right. Their delicate flavour bears out the old adage: 'Steady the basses; give the tenors a chance . . .'

It is unthinkable nowadays that anyone should take seriously a recipe in which truffles were combined with anchovy fillets. It is, however, the case of pheasant *à la Sainte Alliance*. The addition in Nîmes or Avignon of the local Vaucluse truffles to classical dishes such as *brandade de morue* (salt cod) is more of an advertisement than an improvement on the original dish.

A truffle is a visible sign of wealth. I had an odd experience in Périgord in 1966. Everywhere I went I would order *oeufs brouillés aux truffes*, truffled scrambled eggs. I tasted one or two mixtures which were good because of the abundance of truffles, but not once was I offered a classic dish of scrambled eggs. One might therefore deduce that the truffle was in itself the justification of any dish!

The aphrodisiac connotations of the truffle might account for the vogue which it enjoyed at a period when people were bored. Perhaps for this reason, certain self-styled gastronomes made a habit of scattering them everywhere. It is true to say that there are few occasions on which they are not appreciated but they are nonetheless better kept in reserve for one's finest dishes and greatest successes. In the modern kitchen, truffles are most closely associated with eggs, salads, poultry and fillet of beef.

To my own way of feeling truffles do have a certain affinity to the making of sauces, though sauces are not their principal domain. On the other hand, bland sauces (eliminating those with a vinegar base such as *miroton* or *charcutière*) are generally all the better for the addition of a touch of truffled stock. A simple béchamel, heightened with truffle stock, develops an incomparable delicacy, as do a *Nantua*, a *capilotade*, a *salmis* or a *blanquette*. The value of this is derived from its use in great moderation. For this reason I am recording a rather amusing recipe – a second recipe inspired by truffles:

SCALLOPS YOKOHAMA (*Coquilles St Jacques Yokohama*)

for each serving:

8-10 scallops
1 dessertspoonful finely-chopped shallots
4 dessertspoonfuls dry white wine
4 dessertspoonfuls fish stock★
salt and cayenne pepper
paprika
saffron
1 egg yolk
2 dessertspoonfuls butter
juice of half a lemon
4 dessertspoonfuls thick cream
truffles
truffle fumet
★in the absence of fish stock substitute
1 dessertspoonful water

Remove the scallops from their shells, wash well and chop. Put into a thick casserole first the chopped shallots, then the scallops seasoned beforehand. Next add the wine and half the butter. Boil this for 2–3 minutes. Remove the scallops and keep them hot on a porcelain serving dish. Reduce the sauce over a brisk fire and pass it through a fine sieve. Add two-thirds of the cream and reduce again.

In a little bowl blend into the yolk of egg a pinch of paprika, a tiny pinch of powdered saffron and a dessertspoonful of lemon juice. The whole ingenuity of the recipe depends on balancing these two spices. One needs enough paprika to absorb the colour of the saffron and only enough saffron to modify the taste of the sauce. (An original sauce is not successful if the trained gastronome can detect and separate its ingredients.)

Next add the liaison prepared above to the casserole and without an instant's delay bring it to the boil and remove from the fire. Stir in the rest of the butter, add a touch of salt if it is needed, pour the sauce over the scallops and serve.

Let us now refashion this recipe to profit by the presence of truffles. The same ingredients are required, with the exception of the paprika and saffron. Greater discretion should also be exercised with the lemon juice and pepper. If the fish *fumet* is available, then reduce the white wine used by half. The truffled liquid should be put into the sauce at the very start; the truffles, or slices of truffle, should be placed on the scallops which are being kept hot. There is a subtlety in their combination which ennobles the sauce.

Certainly if you are lucky enough one day to find yourself with a lot of truffles on your hands you can just sauté them along with some scallops and the results will be far from displeasing. By comparison with the recipe outlined above, however, it is only a workman's dish – a workman from Périgord, of course.

WINE AND SPIRITS

For the making of a good sauce, good wine is essential. Obviously one hesitates to 'sacrifice' a great bottle to a *civet*, but one is wrong unless the bottle is a genuine rarity or, through its age, is too light. Sauces are better made with round, full wines than with light ones.

Red wine sauces undoubtedly take precedence over white wine ones,

Sauces for Burgundian Fondue (*Sauces pour Fondue Bourguignonne*)

and hardly any sauce is made with *vin rosé*. *Vin mutté* wines give good results, as do Muscat de Frontignan, Banyuls, Picardan and others made from the *grenache* grape, while Champagne makes very elegant sauces for fish and white meat. I have, however, always been aware of the great difference in quality between sauces made with white wine and those made with red. I am positive that red wines do not lose their quality in sauces but, alas, that white wines do. In my time I have made many trial sauces with Sauternes using for the purpose the very finest vintages but achieving only indifferent results. On the other hand, the finest *civet* that I ever ate had been moistened – this was in 1958 – with a Haut Brion 1945. I still remember a guest who claimed that the lamprey served at St Emilion was better than in my native Langon because, he said, the wine was better there. This completely exasperated my father who never used any wine for lamprey other than St Emilion or Pomerol. It was as though a cook should refuse in Bordeaux to make use of a Burgundy, or vice versa.

As for spirits, of whatever kind, their use in the kitchen must be extremely discreet in order that their aggressive character shall never be traced in a sauce. Largely for this reason one sets them alight. Many cooks – particularly those with a too-sharp eye for a profit – have observed that a spirit used at the start of a dish (and especially of a sauce) and then fired leaves a much more discreet trace of its presence than does a much smaller quantity of the same spirit added at the last moment. For this reason it is legitimate to suppose that a Madeira sauce strongly redolent of Madeira is more than likely to contain only a eyedropful of Madeira added at the last possible moment. On the other hand, there has for some time existed a school of *'flambeurs'* (inveterate arsonists) who have made the abuse of spirits and pepper a substitute for technical skill. The making of sauces starts from a totally alien but everyday idea. *Flamber*, to fire, is to strengthen and solidify meat by means of a simple physical process: the brutal but brief excess of heat. It goes without saying that the flavour of the spirit concerned plays a part in the dish, but a very restrained part, and its place of origin is more important than its age or its aristocracy. This is one of the reasons why I tend to use young Armagnac above all. The grounds for this will be obvious to anyone who knows the basic difference between Armagnac and Cognac. Armagnac, is richer in 'ethers' which are admirable when released by fire.

It is curious to record that other spirits give much less reliable results,

Breast of Veal with Pimentos (*Tendrons de Veau aux Piments Forts*)

including *marc* which, after all, is another form of distillation but one still based on grapes. The fashion for whisky has led to a whole series of pyrotechnical dishes: chickens, lobsters, entrecôtes. The conscientious cook, however, tends to mix whisky with brandy (as opposed to Cognac) in order to achieve better results. Brandy, which is distilled from wines of no

certified origin, can serve just as well as Armagnac if of good quality, which is certainly possible.

Much thought has been given to the best marriage of garnishes with alcohol for flaming, hence the origin of *Poulet Vallée d'Auge* and *Canard aux Pommes* where Calvados is used for lighting and applies as a garnish. It would be idle to criticize this approach because it springs on one hand from a spirit of enquiry and on the other from the pursuit of something fresh, both equally laudable.

It must nevertheless be admitted that there are in practice no sauces based on alcohol. A small number of restaurateurs have attempted a *zabaglione* sprinkled with *eaux de vie* (*poire, kirsch, mirabelle,* etc.) using it to demonstrate their own virtuosity in the dining-room and face to face with their clients. The spectacle hardly justifies the resultant indigestion.

To sum up, it should be stated that spirits can only be used as a supplementary element in sauces, in precisely the same terms as a spice or herb. This is a complete contrast with the use to be made of wine, cider or beer. The ability of the sauce-cook is to be measured in terms of his restraint.

FILLETS OF JOHN DORY IN WHITE WINE (*Filets de St Pierre au Vin Blanc*)

Illustrating the use of a white wine sauce.

6 servings:

a 5 lb. John Dory
5 oz. shallots
½ pint (1¼ cups) dry white wine
juice of 1 lemon
½ pint (1¼ cups) water
1 large onion, chopped
salt
liaison:
2 dessertspoonfuls thick cream
3 egg yolks
2 oz. (¼ cup) butter
salt and pepper

Fillet the fish and strip off the skin. Put all the fish except the fillets into a casserole with the chopped onion, the water and the wine. Boil for 10 minutes and pass through muslin or a fine sieve. Cover the bottom of a well-buttered dish with finely-chopped shallots. Place on top of them the fillets cut into 6 or 12 portions. Add salt sparingly. Cover the whole with well-buttered tinfoil. Add the fish bouillon and cook for 5–6 minutes over a moderate flame.

Dry the fillets on a serving dish. Pass the sauce through muslin. Pour it into a thick-bottomed saucepan and set it over a hot flame. Reduce by one-third or more if need be. Add the cream and reduce a little more. Stir the lemon juice into the yolks and add a little of the hot sauce from the saucepan so as to avoid making scrambled eggs. Add this mixture to the pan and bring to the boil, beating constantly. At the moment of boiling withdraw the pan from the fire and at the last moment correct the seasoning if necessary. Finally stir in the butter very gradually. Cover the fillets with the sauce and serve.

POACHED EGGS AND LEEKS IN RED WINE (*Oeufs Pochés à la Marinette*)
Illustrating the use of red wine.
6 servings:

12 eggs
1 bottle of a young and powerful red wine
salt, pepper, nutmeg
$1\frac{1}{4}$ lb. white stems of leeks, cut into sections of $1\frac{1}{2}$ in.
2 oz. ($1\frac{1}{4}$ cups) butter
2 fl. oz. ($\frac{1}{4}$ cup) oil
sauce:
6 slices of bread, trimmed
1 oz. ($\frac{1}{8}$ cup) butter
1 fl. oz. ($\frac{1}{8}$ cup) olive oil
1 dessertspoonful flour

Pour one-third of the red wine into a casserole and poach the eggs in it one by one until they are hard. Let them dry off in a cloth or a plate. Where necessary for the poaching add more wine. This should be seasoned with pepper and nutmeg, but no salt. One can also omit the nutmeg and substitute 6 cloves. At the end of this stage, keep the eggs in a temperate place (above the stove, for instance).

Remove the remaining wine from the casserole and keep on one side, add the butter and oil and simmer the pieces of leek in it until they are well browned. Add a dessertspoonful of flour and let it brown. Return the cooking wine to the pan and add the remainder, a little salt and cook for 20 minutes. Cut roundels from the bread big enough to fit the eggs. Fry them in oil and butter and set them out on a serving plate. Place the poached eggs on top and cover them with the boiling sauce. Serve at once.

SOME UNCLASSIFIED SAUCES

ALBERT
This is the French name for the English horseradish sauce. It can be made with breadcrumbs, cream and grated horseradish, or with a béchamel

sauce, or with cream and horseradish alone. It is most commonly served with roast beef.

AMIRAL
For boiled fish. A butter sauce, which includes anchovies, chives and capers as well as a little lemon peel. Lemon juice is added with the seasoning when the sauce is cooked.

BÂTARDE
For vegetables and boiled fish. Flour and butter blended together, salted water, egg yolks and melted butter are the ingredients. Lemon juice may be added at the last moment.

CHAPELURE
Sauce chapelure or *à la chapelure* is the French version of the English bread sauce. Carême gives a recipe in which chopped shallots are simmered in

light veal stock and pepper; breadcrumbs are added when the shallots are cooked, together with butter and lemon juice. The classic English sauce, however, is made with milk, onions, cloves, mace, cream, butter, salt and pepper.

À L'ESTRAGON

There are different versions of tarragon sauce depending upon the dish with which it is to be served. For eggs and small cuts of meat it is usually made with white wine and tarragon leaves cooked together, added to a reduced veal stock and strained. For sauté meat and poultry, the liquid in which the dish has been cooked is moistened with white wine; chopped tarragon leaves and stock are added and the liaison is made with *beurre manié*. For boiled chicken, tarragon leaves are added to the chicken stock when the bird is cooked; the sauce being thickened after reduction.

GÉNOISE

This is an old name for *sauce Genevoise* (*see* page 54).

MOELLE

A variation of *sauce Bordelaise*, using white wine instead of red and with the addition of diced bone marrow.

NEWBURG

For hot lobster. This American sauce has become particularly associated with Lobster Newburg. It is a hot emulsified sauce made from butter, sherry, cream, yolks of eggs and paprika and salt for seasoning.

PIQUANTE

A white wine sauce generally served with left-over meats. Chopped onions, pickles or gherkins, flour, chopped chervil, parsley and tarragon are the ingredients as well as gravy or liquid from the meat.

PROVENÇALE

For egg or fish, small cuts of meat, chicken or vegetables. There are different versions of this sauce, which is made basically from onions or shallots simmered in oil, moistened with meat stock or bouillon. Some versions have mushrooms, others tomatoes, others again have neither. Yet another variation, particularly associated with salmon, includes yolks of eggs and chervil and is cooked like a *sauce Béarnaise* with the oil taking the place of butter.

RAIFORT
Another horseradish sauce, with cream, grated horseradish soaked in milk, seasoned, and with vinegar or lemon juice added at the last moment. In Alsace this may be served with boiled sausages.

VINAIGRETTE
The classic proportions of *sauce vinaigrette* are three parts of oil to one of vinegar. This may be lengthened even further according to taste. Many people today use lemon juice instead of vinegar for certain dishes. As well as with salads, *sauce vinaigrette* may be served with asparagus, cauliflower, fish, with or without herbs, parsley or garlic; it may be seasoned with salt and pepper alone or with the addition of mustard.

IMPROVISATION

If every aspect of the subject of sauces as they appear in every climate and from the dawn of time were to be covered, a ten-volume dictionary would be needed. There is more room for imagination in this branch of cookery than in almost any other. I have repeatedly said that few things can be invented in cookery, and that to create a new recipe it is necessary to make a new product. The adaptation of recipes, especially those for sauces, will give many interesting innovations. I would like to find a formula in which the word innovation would be unimportant. I want to transpose in the musical sense. A Chinese sauce without any soya, one from Vietnam without *Nuoc-mam*, a Mexican sauce without chillies, or a Scandinavian one without fruit preserves, every one of these is a paradox. Although granted that sauces cannot be patented, it will be enough to cut out just one of the ingredients to alter the final result. This is the reason why the Americans, who have brought to a fine art formulas for commercial sauces, are so jealous in guarding their secrets. We all know how to rediscover a taste, but the secret of a recipe does not lie in the taste. The interest lies in the outward aspect, with all that this implies; not only in the colour but in the presentation and, above all, the texture of the dish. Therefore, although obliged by law to publish the formula, the manufacturers take good care not to be very precise. Terms such as 'vegetable oils', 'starchy products', 'carbohydrates' and 'fats' cover a wide range of products prepared by roasting, concentrating, evaporating and so on. So the imitator must be prepared to feel his way in the dark, which may take an unconscionable time. Commercially speaking, this is of the first importance. Chefs who operate on a large scale are well aware of this. It is easy to confuse potato, maize and rice flour starch; reactions to heat, however, will be different. Again, the secret might equally lie in whether the blending agent is cooked or not. When a sauce is successfully prepared, one's distress can be profound when, after cooling and reheating, it becomes a trembling jelly. This is unfortunately all too often the case.

When it comes to inventions, not everything is permitted, except when success justifies the means. Complications are often the result of salvage operations. In making a sauce there is every opportunity for experiment.

Although it is difficult, if not impossible, to rescue a roast, an omelette or many fish dishes from disaster, it is possible to begin a sauce again and yet again. I have explained (*see* page 24) the meaning of the word *décanter*. We can therefore claim to work, fortify, blend, reduce and garnish a sauce several times between decanting and serving it. A mayonnaise can be re-started and yet in the final result will show no trace of this.

On the other hand, it is clear that although there may be nothing new in cookery, new horizons are opening before us thanks to modern technology. The only excuse a housewife would be able to give today for her mayonnaise being a failure would be the absence of an electric mixer. Fireproof casseroles and pans made of glass or enamelled cast iron guarantee success where formerly it would have been a difficult matter. We are now faced with a problem which is at the same time both complicated and very simple, brought about by the possession of modern equipment.

An electric whisk and beater, a blender or mixer, good quality pots and pans, plus an old-fashioned hand whisk and a wooden spoon, are the tools of the modern saucemaker. The conical sieves, strainers, tammy cloths used by our parents have lost some of their importance. As with Cellini's sword, the one universal tool for making cold sauces is the blender. It can be used for all kinds of cold sauces, whether emulsified or not. Of the various forms of bowls, the best ones are those shaped more or less like large tumblers, the square one being the most efficient as the ingredients are thrown against the corners and are therefore blended better.

To make a perfect mayonnaise with a blender the procedure is as follows. Put vinegar, mustard, salt, pepper and yolks of eggs in the bottom of the glass and as much oil as is necessary. Start the blender. Increase the speed and slow it down once or twice during the mixing. This will not take more than a few seconds. Setting the machine up beforehand and cleaning it afterwards takes more time.

An automatic or electric whisk makes it possible for the amateur to prepare mixtures in a saucepan and over the fire which would only be possible for a professional with a hand whisk. Egg yolks, the basis of all emulsions, may now be beaten as well as they possibly can be, thanks to the speed of the mixer.

To sum up, marvellous opportunities now lie before the amateur, for whom previously many sauce making techniques were beyond his or her reach. It is just these points that we will discuss, assuming that we have kitchen aids, and above all, a blender. The best of these rotate roughly 10,000 times a minute. It is this speed that is responsible for the results obtained. We have seen how to succeed. The making of a mayonnaise has been described; it would be profitable to review this in detail.

Four-fifths of the volume of mayonnaise is oil. Being a fat, its specific gravity is less than that of the other ingredients, and it will therefore float on top. However, as these are mixed very rapidly, separation will only be partial. Sometimes mayonnaises stay liquid after mixing. There is only one cause for this: no vinegar, or water. Normally it will be sufficient to pour in vinegar; let it sink to the bottom, wait for a few minutes and start the blender again. Sometimes this rescue operation can go wrong. When this happens, pour the mayonnaise out of the blender and make a very small quantity of fresh mayonnaise, using one egg yolk, a very little vinegar and salt, and incorporate a little of the sauce already prepared. Give one or two turns and when the sauce has thickened, add the remainder.

Those demonstrators who, like jugglers, amaze us when they perform at fairs, have found an infallible method. They use whole eggs. This solves all problems. White of egg is one of the blandest of foodstuffs. Its presence in a sauce can do no harm. For an obscure reason, sauces made with a basis of whole eggs are heavier than others. More important to my mind, sauces made from yolks of eggs alone are much more refined, delicate and are a much better colour and texture, which is most important. Also, emulsified sauces made from whole eggs absorb garnishings much less well, although they are less liable to go wrong.

The classical garnishes are gherkins, capers, fresh herbs, tomatoes, shallots. Mustard sauce, *rémoulade*, *tartare*, green sauce, *mousquetaire*, *Tyrolienne*, *sauce Venitienne*, all these can easily be made with modern kitchen equipment.

However, when we come to the realm of fantasy there are many exciting possibilities. Fantasies are those touches of improvization which are not important enough to justify a complete recipe. I would like to make myself clear on this point. I often prepare sauces which appear to be classical, well-documented, well-known ones; this may be purely by chance. To use the phrase dear to novelists, all resemblance to recognized sauces or those in copyright is purely coincidental. It is this aspect which interests me.

I do not know if you are economical, but I am and so are all my family. Left-overs, little bits of this and that carefully put away in saucers and bowls are apt to stay for a long time in my refrigerator. It may be some spinach, brains, a sweetbread, or curry sauce. When I am in the country, I make a sauce every Sunday which is meant to accompany anything from cold meat, hard-boiled eggs, omelettes, macaroni salad or palm hearts to crab. Regardless of what the dinner is going to be, I am always forced to prepare a sauce. Invariably this is a mayonnaise which has tossed into it whatever I happen to find in the refrigerator or larder. There is always something to hand in a jar or bottle – onions, pickles, piccalillis, soya sauce, Worcester sauce, ketchup, chutney. You will probably have spotted a jar of piccalilli or baby onions specially opened for someone which sits about for days almost empty, but no one likes to throw it away. This is not all. You may have some unused whites of eggs, perhaps those whose yolks have been used in a sauce. Cook them in a shallow pan in oil like a pancake, and they can be used up in all sorts of salad dressings.

Be warned, however, because in the following pages none of the recipes I mention will be carefully thought out and planned. Obviously, detailed instructions are necessary for beginners, and explanations will be given. It is helpful to lay down basic guiding rules. Do not have preconceived ideas. The affinity of some materials to others may seem perfectly obvious yet hard to rationalize.

I have tried hard, but unsuccessfully, to simplify the list of ingredients. For example, I have attempted to standardize and to be consistent in giving certain weights. In making roux, for example, the weights of flour and butter should, generally speaking, be equal. This is much better than always trying to give precise weights. To do this would only be really useful in those particular instances where the chemical composition of the farinaceous substance exactly corresponds with the liquidity and purity of the fat used. This must be taken into account as well as the quality of the flour and butter. Since we are concerned with sauces and above all with small quantities of sauces, such precision is worthless. What is important is that one must use one's own judgement in making a sauce. So in the following recipes you will find broad outlines and general indications. I could not give you all the recipes possible in my system. I can only describe my experiments which, I must confess, have often given much pleasure.

Picture me then in my kitchen, with the refrigerator beside the larder. Perishable foodstuffs in the one, all sorts of bottles of condiments in the other. Let us start by taking a particular example. I have the remains of a curry with some pieces of meat in it. The sauce I have in mind is to accompany cold meats and hard-boiled eggs. So I put the curry (carefully removing any bones from the pieces of meat) into the blender. I add, if I can find some, a little chutney, liquid from a bottle of pimentos, and perhaps two or three little peppers, or maybe a big one. I then add all the usual constituents of a mayonnaise and I turn the blender up to maximum speed in a short burst. I taste, correct the seasoning with salt and pepper;

another mix, and it is ready to serve. Do remember two important things. The sauce must be rather highly seasoned with condiments, mustard being the last one to be put in. I could dwell on the subject of the different varieties and quantities of mustard. For the curry recipe, English mustard should predominate. This, which has a lot of ginger in it, goes best with this mixture. But in general, Dijon mustard, with its strong and aromatic flavour, is the best one to use.

There is another typical peasant or country way of using up remains or left-overs. To do this, heat up the curry with the pieces of meat boned and then mashed, and break an egg or two into it and either leave to cook and then lift them with a fork or stir them all up together. This is an old peasant method, very popular in the centre of France; it is an economical and sensible way of making use of what is left over. This method is called *en oeuf tourné*. However, in a well-organized kitchen, there should not be enough left-overs to justify more elaborate recipes than the one I have just given.

A fact which is not as well known as it should be is that mayonnaise can be finished au gratin perfectly well either in the oven or under a hot grill. It is best mixed with some other ingredient. As an example, here is a recipe for *Langouste à la Corse*.

CRAYFISH CORSICAN STYLE (*Langouste à la Corse*)

1 crayfish weighing between ¾ lb. and 2 lb.
oil
butter
salt, pepper
½ glass Cognac
4 tablespoonfuls mayonnaise

Split the crayfish in two lengthways. Remove the coral and mash it in a bowl with the mayonnaise. Put on one side in a cool place. Warm the oil and butter in a pan; put the crawfish in this and brown on both sides of the two pieces; season with salt and pepper and pour the Cognac over them. Set alight and let all the Cognac burn up. Put the pan in a hot oven for about 10 minutes. Pour away the cooking fat. Coat the open surfaces of the pieces with the mayonnaise and coral mixture, and brown in a hot oven for 10 minutes. Serve very hot immediately.

Again, this may be taken not as a precise recipe but more as a guide to the dish, which may be varied in different ways.

Supposing you have some vegetables you would like to have *gratiné* or browned – asparagus, artichoke hearts, cauliflowers or potatoes. And perhaps you have ready to hand half a set of brains with capers, a couple of slices of cooked tongue, sweetbreads, spinach purée already chopped and cooked in butter, or an artichoke and four or five eggs.

Make a mayonnaise, and then add whatever is available as, for example, sweetbreads or spinach or both of them together. Blend them in the mixer and cover the vegetables with this sauce which will brown beautifully without the addition of cheese. A point to note is that both the vegetables and their dish ought to be hot before being covered with the mayonnaise. The order of this recipe can be reversed; make the sauce with asparagus and pour it over the artichokes or meat scraps.

Now take as an example a sauce meant for pasta salad. This is a good way of using up quite a variety of left-overs. Whites of eggs fried and mashed are one example. But the main constituent of the dish must be borne in mind. If this is to be fish, try to pick out anchovies, sardines, salmon or other fish. If, on the other hand, you want a meat dish, look for sweetbreads, brains, *pâté* or ham. At all events, use whatever you have available. If you have decided on a noodle salad, here is a recipe for one.

NOODLE SALAD MARCO POLO (*Salade Marco Polo*)

4–6 servings:

½ **lb. noodles**
1¾–2½ **pints (2½–3 pints) water**
1 **coffeespoonful coarse salt**
2 **eggs**
1 **small tin of tunny fish (tuna fish)**
3 **fish quenelles**
8 **gherkins**
1 **or 2 bottled peppers**
1 **hard-boiled egg**
4 **tablespoonfuls olive oil**
1 **large tablespoonful mustard**
6 **tablespoonfuls groundnut oil**
4 **tablespoonfuls vinegar**
paprika
cayenne pepper
fine salt

Put the water in a large pot and bring to the boil. Salt, add the noodles stirring with a wooden spoon, and boil vigorously for 6 minutes.

Drain the noodles in a colander and allow them to cool. Place them in a large salad bowl. Dress them with a spoonful of olive oil or groundnut oil; mix thoroughly and add 4 chopped gherkins and the tunny fish, flaked or mashed. Separate the whites and yolks of the eggs. Fry the whites in a little oil like a pancake. Turn over when one side is cooked, slide on to a plate and allow to cool. Place the yolks in a mixing bowl with oil, mustard, vinegar, paprika and salt. Pour into the blender and switch on until the sauce thickens and then pour it over the noodles in the salad bowl.

Cut the fish *quenelles* and the fried whites of eggs in small pieces; add to the salad. Toss the salad and decorate with slices of hard-boiled egg, red peppers and 4 sliced gherkins. Chill before serving.

The variations and adaptations I am going to suggest can be incorporated in the original recipes.

Salmon, uncooked, smoked or poached, can help to make wonderful sauce. The pinkish colour can be deepened with a little tomato, or a sauce sprinkled or dotted with roe. A sauce for a lettuce or palm heart salad can be truly memorable with avocado pear blended in it. A sauce with sardines is perfectly acceptable with a tomato salad.

Sauces with a lot of herbs such as sorrel or cress are very delicate. Cress and sorrel can be used uncooked, or they may be cooked in butter, left to cool and then used. If this is done, it is a good idea to add enough parsley to make the sauce a fresh green, which does not happen with cooked cress and sorrel. But there are no strict rules and anything is permissible.

If you are making a salad which includes something solid, there is just one inconvenience, which is that the sauce must not be added to the dish until the right moment.

It is obvious that if a sauce is very rich all it needs is a framework. Pasta salads or potato *gratiné* dishes are examples of this. The salad which for lack of a better name we call Lyonnaise is an excellent one. This is composed of lettuce or endive or chicory and the sauce is made as follows. Mash or slice hard-boiled eggs, add salt and pepper, ground walnuts and chicken livers stewed in butter until they are brown outside but still a delicate pink inside, Dijon mustard, oil and vinegar. The oil can be a mixture of oils or one alone. At harvest time, we use a mixture of walnut and groundnut oils. But generally a good quality olive oil gives excellent results. All these are mixed, not in the bottom of the salad bowl with spoon and fork, but in the mixer. This makes a delicious rich smooth thickened sauce. As I am going to discuss salad sauces and dressings in detail, I want to say that I prefer the latter method. The clinging quality of mayonnaise gives the best results when the dressing is for immediate use.

The importance of small things must be emphasized. Salad dressings are prepared in the bottom of the salad bowl. Salt, pepper come first and then are dissolved in a little vinegar. Then the mustard follows, hard-boiled eggs, cheese, ham, whatever the choice is. Not until then should the rest of the vinegar be added and last of all, the oil. Mix everything together and then put the salad on top, and toss it all together.

This operation is sometimes known as *fatiguer*, literally 'to tire' a salad, which is then *cuit* or 'cooked'. In this jargon, a 'cooked' salad is one which is left several hours to rest after being seasoned and mixed. Such a salad is hardly prepossessing or appetizing. Some amateurs support this theory. Often salads of this sort are being served for the second time, a relic of our grandparents' parsimonious and economical habits, allowing nothing to be wasted. This method is only possible at all with a *vinaigrette* dressing, as in the same circumstances, a mayonnaise will disintegrate.

If you are preparing a salad with mayonnaise, or for that matter, any cold emulsified sauce, do not make it until the very last moment. For a *vinaigrette*, it is not quite so important, and it does not harm the salad to wait some twenty minutes. But with a mayonnaise, even a few minutes will be enough to spoil everything. Mayonnaise will liquefy in contact with water. Now a salad, if dried correctly, must still be a little damp else it will be bruised. To make this kind of salad, you must work in topsy-turvy fashion, putting the salad in the bowl first and then pouring the dressing on top. In either case, do not toss until the last moment.

It is quite the reverse with a pasta salad, which has been previously cooked, strained and dressed with oil. Here there is no risk of failure, and in fact the mixing of the sauce with the salad tends to thicken it. If the sauce becomes too thick it is a simple matter to add some lemon juice, vinegar or water to correct this.

Sauces will react differently according to the nature of the substances they accompany. So a *Périgueux* sauce served on a steak ought to be subtly different from the same sauce with celery hearts braised in butter, if the maximum pleasure and advantage is to be gained. Blended sauces marry best with steaks. But a vegetable, which must be slightly wet if it is to preserve its flavour and suppleness, calls for a thicker sauce and one which, to use an expressive term, *nappe*, i.e. blankets the dish. The sauce must be pulled together (*reserré, see* page 31) which means that, in this case, it must be thickened with a little potato flour or cornflour dissolved in a dessertspoonful of port, sherry or Madeira. It must not be forgotten that a sauce should not be too thick. The difficulty lies in judging the proper thickness of a sauce in relation to what it is accompanying.

But let us return to salad dressings. These are usually called *vinaigrettes*, a simple basis of oil, vinegar, salt and pepper being all that is required for the simplest of them. I have already said that the salt and pepper can be dissolved in the vinegar before adding the oil. Many housewives put the seasoning in a spoon, then add a little vinegar and whisk with a fork before turning out into the bowl. Others claim that the salt dissolves better in the oil and work the other way round. I do not think it makes any difference. I do not think it is at all important, but if you want to be on the safe side, you may dissolve the salt in water, the amount of which depends on the quantity of salad or dressing. What is of fundamental importance is the ratio of oil to vinegar. This is generally accepted as being three times as much oil as vinegar, that is one spoonful of vinegar to three of oil. It is not an absolute rule, but is pretty close to the truth. There are vinegars and vinegars, Aromatic vinegar is made of *alcoolat vulnéraire*, or rose petal vinegar, made from crushing 2 oz. rose petals in a pint of vinegar and leaving them for ten days to soak. Or fill a stoneware crock with freshly-picked raspberries, cover with vinegar and leave for a week, strain through a cloth (but do not press). Some vinegars are very strong, others mild. In former times it used to be the practice to blend new wine with an old one of good quality, cork it and leave in the sun in clear glass vats. Today, the commercial manufacturers of vinegar argue 'why should anyone buy water?' So the tendency is to fortify the vinegar with extracts, it being easier to lengthen an ordinary vinegar than to concentrate it. This is abandoning delicacy in favour of strength. An old home-made vinegar, aromatic but light, will do much more for a seasoning than a commercial product. It is toward this sort of product that the sauce maker must turn If we take into account the very small amount of vinegar used in cold emulsified sauces in comparison to that in hot ones, we must be confident about this difference.

Manufacturers of commercial sauces tried to stabilize them by using colloidal agents, to maintain the mixture in a state of particular suspension. Gelatine or starches were essential. Nowadays all this is unnecessary. If it is absolutely essential, raw or cooked yolks of eggs will give satisfactory results. It is amusing to note how often there is confusion between some sauces, for instance between a *rémoulade* and a *tartare*. In many popular restaurants, celery *rémoulade* (strictly speaking a mustard sauce) is quite plainly mayonnaise, and it is rare to find a *sauce tartare* which is not simply a near-mayonnaise.

I have always been of the opinion that certain sauces do not marry well with herbs. I would be unwilling to add them to a *blanquette* or to a Marco Polo salad. I am assured that this is not against the rules, but I seem to be alone in this.

As their name indicates, *vinaigrette* sauces contain vinegar. The vinegar is a seasoning in itself, so other fats can be substituted for oil. In Savoy and Dauphiné cream is used; in the south-west, goose fat, to be precise the oil which forms on the surface of the fat. In many remote parts of France pork fat is used for a dandelion salad. I do not speak of the substitutes which were used in times of restrictions, such as quince jelly or apple pectin. Salad dressings are all derived from a mixture of oil and vinegar. As I have said about all the other sauces, it is the united qualities of all the elements present in the sauce which determine the final success. Oils which hold the tang of unripe nuts will ruin the best of vinegars. It must also be borne in mind that vinegar is not the only acid which can be used for seasoning salad dressings. Lemon or lime juice may be an excellent choice. But with these remember the relative proportions, as vinegar is often much more acid than lemon juice.

Garnishes must also be taken into consideration. Salads garnished with diced cheese, chopped scarlet pickled tongue, quartered hard-boiled eggs, or slices of avocado, will all need different quantities of these ingredients. This should never be more than the volume of the dressing.

I have never been completely in agreement with those gastronomes who believe that a dressing must only be made on the spot, at the last moment. Not that I have anything against the system, but I hold that it is not very important. A *vinaigrette* may be perfectly well prepared, with extreme refinement, and then successfully served when needed, after being vigorously tossed and mixed. This dressing will keep perfectly well, provided that it does not stand indefinitely in a jar or a terrine. To make this sauce means taking an infinity of trouble; amateurs generally leave it to the restaurateurs, blaming any mediocrity in their results on the system as a whole, although in fact it is a sign of their own inefficiency as cooks.

Those who make sauces in public do so with a deal of flourish and display. They do this not in the bottom of the salad bowl, which would be invisible to everyone but the performer, but in the open, as it were, on a flat plate. Garlic is crushed with a fork, a little yolk of egg mashed into mustard, lemon juice is added here and a drop of vinegar there, the oil and tabasco elegantly mixed; it is all quite a spectacle.

Nevertheless, everyone to his taste. The field is large and we have yet to discover the perfect salad dressings (wherein the golden number plays an important role) or the forgotten recipe on the Obelisk of Luxor.

MUSTARD SAUCE (*Sauce Rémoulade*)

$1\frac{3}{4}$ pints ($2\frac{1}{2}$ pints) mayonnaise
$1\frac{1}{2}$ tablespoonfuls French
mustard
$1\frac{1}{2}$ oz. gherkins
1 tablespoonful chopped
parsley
chopped chervil and
tarragon
$\frac{1}{2}$ tablespoonful anchovy
essence

Add all the ingredients to the mayonnaise
and mix.

SAUCE TARTARE

8 yolks of eggs
salt, pepper
$1\frac{3}{4}$ pints ($2\frac{1}{4}$ pints) oil
2 tablespoonfuls vinegar
about 1 oz. spring onions
and chives
2 tablespoonfuls mayon-
naise

Boil the eggs hard and mash the yolks in
a terrine; work them into a soft paste.
Season well with salt and freshly-ground
pepper. Work in the oil and then the
vinegar. Finish off with the chives and
onions, cut up so finely that they become
a sort of purée, fold the mayonnaise,
pound, and strain through a cloth. This
sauce goes happily with cold chicken or
cold meat and also with devilled chicken
or meat.

SAUCES
FROM OUTSIDE FRANCE

BELGIUM

WATTERZOÏ

Watterzoï, like Aphrodite, was born in a storm – that is, chicken Watterzoï, which was originally a fish soup. The following recipe is therefore no longer an accompanying sauce, but one containing both solids and liquid. I know that nobody would take this to be a national dish although such an error might not be unreasonable, since it is considered a minor masterpiece in its native country.

1 chicken
butter
oil
salt, pepper
leeks and celery
sprigs and roots of parsley
1 onion stuck with cloves
¾ pint (1 pint) cream
4 egg yolks
chervil sprigs
croûtons of bread
fennel root

Cut the chicken in pieces and put in a *cocotte* with some butter and hot oil. Colour and season. Chop a few of the leeks and some celery sticks. Put them in another pan and cook gently until they colour and become translucent. Add the chicken pieces, moisten with a little water. Add the parsley, onion and seasoning. Simmer with the lid on until the chicken is cooked. Add more water as necessary to maintain the liquid level and more seasoning in proportion. Cut the remainder of the leeks and celery into tiny cubes. Season and put into separate pans with butter.

When the chicken is cooked, put the pieces in a shallow dish with the chopped vegetables and a little of their liquid. Keep hot. Strain the remaining liquid from the vegetables and bring quickly to the boil. Blend this with the fresh cream and yolks of eggs, previously whisked. Pour this sauce over the pieces of chicken and sprinkle with the chervil. Garnish with the croûtons fried in butter and oil. Eat this dish hot in shallow bowls.

As a variation on this recipe, I created the following chicken dish, named in honour of my friend Emmanuel Berl.

CHICKEN EMMANUEL BERL (*Poulet Emmanuel Berl*)

1 chicken, about 2¾ lb.
over ¼ lb. leek stems
under ½ lb. celery
1 fennel heart
3 garlic cloves
½ French loaf
bouquet garni
2 oz. butter
1 dessertspoonful oil
bunch of parsley
water
salt
about 10 fl. oz. (1¼ cups) cream
4 egg yolks
1 teaspoonful ground rice
pinch of cayenne pepper
croûtons of bread

Joint the chicken and cut the joints in half. Cut the carcass in 3 or 4 pieces. Put in a stewpan with butter and warm oil. Season and cook gently until the pieces colour. Now chop the leeks, celery and fennel and put in another pan with warmed butter. Stir with a wooden spoon and season lightly.

When the chicken pieces are golden-brown, drain them and put into the pan containing the vegetables. Add the bouquet garni, pounded garlic and bunch of parsley. Stir gently with the wooden spoon. Add water, cover and cook gently.

Beat the cream with the egg yolks and ground rice. Season with cayenne pepper. Take the parsley out of the pan, put on a tammy cloth, and rub with a pestle or spoon handle, crushing it completely. First stretch the cloth over a bowl or jug to catch the juice as it drips through the cloth. Add this juice to the egg and cream mixture. Take the chicken pieces from the pan and arrange on the serving dish. Blend the egg and cream mixture with the sauce, stir and pour into a tureen.

Toast the croûtons of bread. Serve in shallow bowls, the chicken first, then the croûtons, and finally the sauce.

Why may one replace fish by chicken in Ostend and not in Marseilles? In Marseilles there are egg, cod and spinach *bouillabaisses*, but God forbid

the domestic fowl! I believe this to be a lesson in Mediterranean psy-
chology. The Belgians in their wisdom adapt their folklore to suit their
needs.

ENGLAND

MINT SAUCE

Little remains to be said after saying that mint sauce is an occasion for
humour. What amuses the French cook is the mere fact of calling this
mixture a sauce.

There was mint in my great-grandfather's garden. What it could be used
for I never knew as I never saw anybody but myself pick it. I was still very
young when I used to prepare a brew in which mint leaves played a pre-
ponderant role. For its preparation a bottle was used, which in itself was
exciting, as one had to be able to hide it. My great-grandfather never
liked anyone to play in his flower beds. It was easy enough to sneak lumps
of sugar off my grandmother's coffee table in the Café de France. This left
only the problem of finding the secondary ingredients which to me really
made the brew. Having been suckled on readings of the *Lettres de Mon
Moulin*, Père Gauchet's elixir was something special. There used to be a
cask of thin wine in the stable loft and over it a damp covering. This wine
made a wonderfully fresh drink. I stuffed the mint leaves into a bottle with
the sugar which I had crumbled; a few drops of water dissolved it. I
stamped them down with a little cane. The bottle was a squat one with a
cork specially fashioned for me secretly by an apprentice. I shook it
vigorously. Then came the most difficult part, namely filling the bottle
with thin wine. I was not allowed to get at the wine, and so the filling was
not without its dangers. There is nothing easier than taking out a spigot,
but it is quite a different matter putting it back. With all possible precaution and a great deal of anxiety, I would undertake this delicate operation. Success achieved, I would rejoin my playfellows with a bottle of
nectar very similar to the mint sauce of my British friends. And to think

that Philip Harben once suspected me of not knowing how to make it – I, who at the age of five and in the most clandestine manner re-invented this sauce – this is an allegation hard to stomach!

In truth, I do not think that mint sauce can undergo any revolutionary transformation. No more do I think that it is desirable that one should make it at all. I am sure that the very British John Cradock (the estimable husband and partner of Madame Bon Viveur) could not find any great poetry in mint sauce.

To return to mint sauce. To everyone who was astonished at my pleasure in living in England, I pointed out that this was entirely my father's fault, he being an uncritical anglophile. Without fully making me share this point of view, he made me go to English schools for several years where, clothed in a uniform and called by an anglicized version of my name, I spent my time unnoticed. This period brought me many new joys and fresh pleasures, among which I do not however count mint sauce, as it was already in my repertoire. But great were the joys of the fish-and-chip shops (*les boutiques de friture*) in Southend, Westcliff or Leigh-on-Sea. I learned to enjoy the coloured lemonade which enhanced our Bank Holidays, the acid drops, the butterscotch and the marshmallows, of which I never had enough. Childhood plays a part in our adult life, above all in matters of taste, which one must not underestimate.

MINT SAUCE

2 oz. mint leaves	Mince or chop the mint leaves very finely.
1 oz. caster sugar	Spoon into a sauce boat add the sugar.
3 oz. vinegar	Pour the boiling water over this. Chill
pinch of salt	and season before serving with hot or
pepper	cold roast lamb.
4 tablespoonfuls boiling water	

INDIA

CURRY

Curious as it may seem, it was not in the sub-continent of India that I ate the best curry; in fact, I have memories of horrible experiences in Karachi and Bombay. But curry is king in Indonesia and throughout all the Far East. Recipes for it fall into two parts: for the curry powder itself (made of root ginger, mace and up to ten other spices) and the meat, chicken or vegetables; together they make up the curry. The results vary both according to the number and quality of the ingredients used, and on the balance of their proportions. With this kind of composite spice one may consider the possibility of the use of the 'golden number'. Cocteau, above all, held that this could not be determined and could only ratify a success very roughly as trial by ordeal did in other connections.

The English, having been in India for two hundred years, proclaimed Victoria Empress in 1870 and introduced curry to the cuisine of France. Two schools of thought have their disciples, one favouring 'brown' curry and the other 'white'. There was a tradition of French-Indian cooking, mainly derived from the colony of Pondicherry, which remained in French hands until quite recently – all that remained of Dupleix' eighteenth-century conquests. This school of cookery favoured a very much cooler and paler curry than the Anglo-Indian recipes. To be absolutely fair, I must admit that I have never seen light-coloured curry in the East or Far East. It seems that the formula *curry à la crème* must be western.

There is a certain amount of confusion over curry in the west, as rice has become so implicit in the dish that this may even be carried to the point that the curry spicing has become no more than an accessory. The origin of the word curry is uncertain, but it is generally admitted to be derived from the Tamil word *kari*, meaning simply, sauce. Today the definition of curry is quite clear. It is a compound of powdered spices containing turmeric, and its use is world wide.

In good restaurants in France, curry is very largely made according to Escoffier's methods.

INDIAN CURRY SAUCE

Stew in a pan with a closely-fitted lid (*see étuver*, page 27) chopped onions, a bunch of parsley with a few sprigs of parsley in it as well, a little mace and cinnamon. Sprinkle with a teaspoonful of curry powder,* moisten it with ¾ pint (1 pint) coconut milk, add the same amount of velouté, plain or rich according to whether the sauce will be used for meat or fish, and leave it to simmer gently for 15 minutes. Strain through a cloth and make up the quantity with 4 fl. oz. (½ cup) of cream and a few drops of lemon juice.

N.B. To obtain this amount of coconut milk, grate about 1½ lb. of fresh coconut and blend it with about 5 fl. oz. (⅓ pint) of tepid milk, strain through a coarse cloth rubbing it hard. If coconut milk is not obtainable, substitute the same quantity of almond milk. Indian cooks prepare this sauce in a variety of ways, but the basic method is always the same. But even if we have the genuine formula it would by and large be unacceptable to most French people. The method given above, which is adapted to European tastes, is better.

(A. Escoffier, Le Guide Culinaire, 1928)

*This will be too little for Anglo-Saxon tastes. (Ed. note)

FRENCH-INDIAN CURRY

2 lb. lean mutton
1 large onion
salt, pinch of curry powder
1½ oz. flour
6 fl. oz. (¾ cup) coconut milk
2 cooking apples

Cut the mutton in small cubes of about 1½ inches square. Brown in pork fat till the meat is tender, add the onion, previously chopped, salt and a pinch of curry powder. When the onion begins to colour, sprinkle with the flour. Cook for a moment, add the coconut milk and simmer gently for 1 hour 30 minutes; 10 minutes before serving, add the apples, peeled, cored and diced. Heap on a serving dish and serve with boiled rice.

To prepare the coconut milk, cut a whole coconut in two and take out the meat. Pound or grate this and add water to cover. Leave to soak for 1 hour. Pile the pulp in a coarse cloth and wring to extract the milk. If dried coconut is used first soak in warm water.

There are many variations. My father made curry as closely as possible to his sacrosanct formula – that is, plenty of onions, cooked till tender in fat with garlic. He added curry powder, browned it and cooked for a moment. He called this operation '*singer*', which term generally means to thicken a sauce with flour.

The meat, whether sautéed or not, was added and it was then moistened with white wine, tomato pulp or fresh tomato sauce, blatantly seasoned and then cooked with a very large bouquet garni. Rice was served separately. There was neither coconut milk nor cooking apples. Today, my own procedure is as follows:

CURRY

$\frac{1}{2}$ **lb. meat**
$\frac{1}{4}$ **lb. chopped onion**
$\frac{2}{3}$ **oz. garlic**
1 tablespoonful curry powder
1 wineglassful coconut milk
1 cooking apple
2$\frac{1}{2}$ oz. lard
cream
oil

Dice the meat, which may be either lamb, chicken or mutton, and fry it until tender and remove from the pan. Chop onions and a little garlic; gently simmer in oil until translucent. As soon as the onions are cooked, add the diced apple. Return the meat to the pan, add the curry powder and reduce by simmering over a low heat for about 20 minutes. Stir in the coconut milk, a bouquet garni and seasoning. Simmer a little more, remove the bouquet garni and blend lightly with a little cream.

Rice is the usual accompaniment to curry. For some people it is indispensable. I myself do not think that the presence of Bombay duck (tiny dried fish) makes any difference to the quality of the curry. Grated coconut, *cacahuettes* (peanuts), sliced and grilled chopped onion or chives, chutney, paprika in oil, chopped eggs, grated vegetables, chuppatis, poppadums, these can all be rated as frills. To be sure, rice is traditionally served with curry, but this is only a habit.

The presence of apples presents no problem as there are apples in season all the year round. However, some chefs replace them with bananas. The coconut milk used in tropical countries is very different from that obtained in Europe. In the tropics it comes from unripe nuts, which are practically full of an opalescent and acid liquid. When in Europe we crush the *copua* and boil it with water or milk and drain off the juice, the result is bound to be imperfect.

Moreover, if we analyse the whole corpus of oriental methods, we discover that sugar plays a part in the preparation of curry. There is not a lot of it, just a touch. For many of us, mango chutney (which is nothing more than a kind of preserve), is indispensable. Apples or bananas are also much appreciated, as they bring a suggestion of sweetness very helpful to highly flavoured dishes.

We discover in this recipe all the oriental secular tradition. The rice is justified by being in keeping with the traditional character of oriental civilization. Curry is a recipe belonging to civilized world cookery.

ITALY

SAUCE BOLOGNESE
Neapolitan, Bolognese, Piedmontese, Venetian, Roman . . . to mention a recipe for an Italian sauce means quarrelling not only with your best friends, but with all the upholders of the 'one and only true recipe'. Do you not know that Lucullus, governor of Sicily, would only have cooking pots forged by Vulcan on Mount Etna? Was Archimedes perhaps executed by mistake, solely because he did not like beans? The gods themselves knew that Italy was the mother country of gastronomy. For all that, is the *sauce Bolognese* which we pour over pasta really anything more than what we have called *sauce hâchée* (literally chopped or minced sauce) for a long time? Liquid cannot be chopped, you tell me. Of course not, but all the ingredients are chopped or minced. As so often in regional cookery, a change of air is enough to change a recipe. In general, truth is not being unduly strained if the central idea is left unaltered, and the spirit of the

dish itself respected. I am tempted to say that *sauce Bolognese* is simply a
well-treated tomato sauce, garnished with sausage skin and chopped mushrooms. It must not be forgotten that a good tomato sauce consists of
softened onions, garlic, stewed herbs, olive oil, tomatoes which have been
skinned and had their seeds removed before being pulped, dry white wine,

a selection of spices, and water. This must all be simmered slowly and
reduced at the side of the fire, and then lengthened with a little chicken
stock if the cooking has thickened it too much.

My father, being of Spanish extraction, took great and jealous pains
with tomato sauce. As I went into this subject in some detail in the section
on tomato sauce, I will not repeat it here.

Sauce hâchée can be very good. It may accompany pastas, tagliatelli and
spaghetti without detriment. I am going to give you an authentic *sauce
Bolognese* made with basil and Chianti, but if you find this too complicated
– well, never mind.

SAUCE HÂCHÉE

onions
shallots
garlic
mushrooms
oil
pork fat
chopped ham
sausage skin
a little flour
concentrated tomato
white wine
salt, pepper
bouquet garni
sprig basil

Use plenty of onions, a moderate amount of shallots, a discreet quantity of garlic and a generous one of mushrooms. Put all these ingredients in a heavy pan with oil and a little fat, pork for preference. Stir with a wooden spoon and cook over a moderate heat. When the mixture has taken colour, add chopped bacon to your taste and sufficient sausage to give a spicy taste. Add the concentrated tomato, the white wine, water, pepper and salt; a bouquet garni and a sprig of basil. Leave this to cook gently for 1 hour. Lift out the basil, but do not worry if it has more or less disappeared. Serve on pasta or in any way you please. Minced beef instead of the chopped ham in my recipe may be used; and of course, the classic garnish of Italian pasta dishes; a generous sprinkling of grated Parmesan cheese.

SAUCE BOLOGNESE (1)

1 lb. beef
1 large onion
1 stick celery
2 bay leaves
8 fl. oz. (1 cup) milk
8 fl. oz. (1 cup) red Chianti
1½ oz. tomato paste
3 oz. butter
1 or 2 carrots, according to size
oil
8 fl. oz. (1 cup) water or clear soup

Cut the meat into small pieces; chop the onion and celery. Sauté the carrots and onion in oil, add the bay leaves. Mix together and add the meat. Keep stirring so that the pieces of meat do not stick together. Pour in the wine, and simmer until it has all evaporated.

Add the tomato paste and keep stirring for 3 or 4 minutes. Boil the milk, add and leave to simmer. Reduce for 2 hours at a low heat.

Finally add water or clear soup to make the sauce liquid again.

SAUCE BOLOGNESE (2)

1½ oz. butter
10 oz. beef
¼ lb. button mushrooms
2 tablespoonfuls flour
3 oz. onions
1½ oz. tomato purée
8 fl. oz. (1 cup) white
 Chianti about 1 pint
 (1¼ cups)
 clear or brown stock

Cut the beef into small cubes, chop the onions finely and dust with the flour. Warm the butter and gently sauté the meat, onions, and mushrooms. Add the tomato purée and then the white wine and stock. Leave this mixture until it becomes a soft and tender ragoût.

JAPAN

SOYA SAUCE

Made from fermented soya beans, this has become extremely popular in Japan, although Chinese in origin. Japanese civilization is based on that of Korea. Japanese cookery has two origins; the first local and traditional, the second brought into the country by the Portuguese. *Temoura* was Portuguese in origin.

The soya sauce marketed commercially as a brown liquid is used in a great variety of dishes, and also figures permanently on the dining tables of all classes of society in Japan. The Chinese use it as the base for the glaze used in preparing pork or duck. This glaze, or sweet-sour sauce, is nearly always made with honey, soya sauce and vinegar, or sugar, soya sauce and yellow wine, etc.

The Japanese are much less imaginative, so they mainly used soya sauce neat. To those of us who consider this kind of sauce to be only a condiment, its addition to every dish appears an abuse.

Temoura, however, can be very good, especially when it is made according to the rules. *Sukiyaki* sometimes surprises the foreigner in spite of its genuine quality, just because the taste of the soya sauce distorts and hides the very delicate taste of the meat. At its best the meat is barely cooked.

In Japan every course of the menu, consisting of numerous tiny dishes, is a festival of soya. I have rarely tasted soup as fine as their eel soup; the liver served in each bowl has an exquisitely delicate flavour. But add a teaspoonful of soya and the charm is ruined. Although I much prefer Chinese to Japanese cooking, I am interested in the latter. This stops short, however, at soya sauce. I certainly like it occasionally, but I do think its employment is intolerably abused. I very much like shrimps brushed with soya sauce. The necessity of disguising mediocre cooking is probably the perfect use of a sauce, in itself a symbol.

MEXICO

MOLE

Mexican gastronomy, even today, is said to be Inca-Maya or Aztec in character. This I can well believe. Spanish names are given to certain dishes although these may be actually pre-Colombian. Among these are avocado, turkey, beans, tomatoes, maize, chocolate – to mention only the most important, and all unknown in Europe before the sixteenth century.

All these are so familiar to us that it comes as a shock when Mexicans remind us of their origin. It is a little like the story of Ivan Topoff who invented a string to cut butter. It is a little hard to have to admit that the *cassoulet* saucepans are older than beans. But this is the truth. Among the curiosities of Mexican cookery, after *Taco* and *Tamalé*, these being served moreover with a delicious special sauce, is *mole*. I think that *mole* is undoubtedly Aztec in origin and that in itself it symbolizes the permanence of the culture of these people. Symbolic cookery, which has lost much of its popularity, survives still in the preparation of those mushrooms which cause hallucinations.

I have myself eaten these dishes and I have been completely baffled by reading a romanticized account of experiences with these mushrooms. I do not deny the power of narcotics and their ability to transport us to another world. I know opium smokers who talk to God as I talk to my village priest. I understand the setting and do not deny its importance. However, I prefer the method used by that lovely Mexican who counted more on the excellence of her cooking to achieve erogenous results than on the curiosity which leads to the ritual consumption of raw mushrooms in multiples of seven.

I am still persuaded that *mole* is the best representative of classical Mexican cookery. I am deeply convinced that as maize has been for thousands of years the foundation of the diet of the American continent, dishes made from it do represent local tradition. *Mole* sauce is very characteristic. Among European medieval sauces many had a base of roasted barley or soaked bread. The earliest use of maize in Europe was in the making of flat cakes. This was a link with ancient ritual dishes of the Phoenicians made from *far* or buckwheat. Such cakes were made from millet and called *polenta, cruchades, gaudes* or *millas* and *mique* well before the appearance of maize.

Without any transition or substitution of nomenclature, millet was abandoned in favour of maize. Before being called maize it was known in France as Turkey corn. Throughout the south-west of France it is still called *blat d'Espagne* (Spanish corn). This was a reminder of its original importation into Europe by the Conquistadors.

Here is a recipe for *mole* which I owe to a ravishing Mexican. I also owe to one of her equally enchanting companions my experience of hallucinatory mushrooms.

MOLE

1 large tender turkey
4 lb. fillet of pork
2 lb. chile mulato
$\frac{1}{2}$ lb. raisins
$\frac{1}{2}$ lb. hazel nuts
$\frac{1}{2}$ lb. almonds
$\frac{1}{2}$ lb. prunes
4 oz. chile passilla
4 oz. ajonjoli
$1\frac{1}{2}$ oz. aniseed
$\frac{1}{2}$ oz. cinnamon
$\frac{1}{4}$ lb. tomatoes
1 clove garlic
1 medium-sized onion
2 lb. pork fat
salt

Put the *chile mulato* on one side, taking out the seeds and the veins and opening them out flat like a leaf. Put $\frac{1}{2}$ lb. fat in a very large pan, and fry the hazel nuts and the unpeeled almonds until they are golden. Take care not to burn them, lest the sauce should become bitter. Remove and reserve. Now fry in turn in the same fat the raisins, prunes and lastly the *chile passilla*, taking care that none of them is more than lightly coloured. Now lightly brown on an iron griddle half the *ajonjoli*, and *chile mulato*, cooking them on both sides and being careful not to scorch them. Add half the aniseed. Next put the two kinds of chillies in a bowl of cold water. This is to soften them and make them easier to pound.

Grill the tomatoes without any fat and leave on one side. Now pound in the following order: garlic, onion, almonds, hazel nuts, the other half of the *ajonjoli*, cinnamon, aniseed; add water, little by little, until the mixture becomes a thick and homogenous paste. After this pound separately the raisins, prunes, chillies and finally the tomatoes, adding this mixture to the other and then add the water in which the chillies were soaking, little by little, as before. All this should make a paste as thick and firm as a cake. Put all this on one side while the meat is being prepared. Joint the turkey and cut the meat in small pieces. Take a very large pot, big enough to hold about 20 pints (25 pints) and fry the turkey and the pork in the fat used for frying the ingredients described above, straining the fat and adding it in proportion. Add to it the remainder of the pork fat.

When the meats are quite cooked and ready, draw to one side, and dissolve the paste in 1¼ pints (3 cups) boiling water; let this mixture cook slowly for 1 hour, stirring continuously with a wooden spoon, because it sticks very easily to the pan. By this time the sauce should be fatty and a little bit clotted, like *crème anglaise tournée* (clotted cream). Add the turkey and the meat to this, salt in proportion and add another 6¼ pints (7½ pints) water. Continue to cook, stirring all the while, until the stew is much reduced and it has turned into an extremely thick sauce.

Serve with the rest of the *ajonjoli* sprinkled over it. *Mole* is even better reheated.

Today, faced with the difficulties of preparing such a recipe, many Mexican families buy *mole* prepared commercially. In this case, fry the powder with a little pork fat. Fry the prunes, raisins, almonds and 1 lb. almonds prepared as in the recipe above, and put everything into an electric blender. Add stock, a bar of chocolate, a little powdered sugar and salt.

NORTH AFRICA

COUSCOUS

The success of *couscous* throughout France today cannot leave the gourmet indifferent. It cannot be denied that great composite dishes belong to the category of sauces; examples are *zarzuela, bouillabaisse* and all sorts of stews and ragoûts made from fish or meat.

The popular liking for this form of gastronomy has tended to reduce a whole meal to a single course. For my part, if this does not become an absolute rule, I feel that it has something to be said for it. May a dish like *couscous* be given as an example? I hardly think so, although it may be possible. Nearly always *couscous* is accompanied by a highly spiced sauce, the equivalent of *rouille* with *bouillabaisse*. The many varieties of this sauce are usually called *Arissa*. Basically this is made from pounded paprika (pimento) and oil. Different ingredients give a personal touch to the sauce. Those mostly used in North Africa are concentrated tomato paste, garlic, fennel, basil, coriander, saffron and so on. These are either mixed together and lengthened with olive oil or marinated with olive oil which has had pimento previously stirred into it.

3 lb. shoulder of mutton
2 lb. chicken
3 courgettes, 3 leeks
1 lb. carrots, 1 lb. turnips
salt, red pepper
30 coriander seeds
3 sprigs arab parsley
pinch of paprika
½ lb. (1 cup) semolina
1 lb. chick peas
1 lb. onions
1½ oz. raisins
pinch of cumin seed
1 ladleful Arissa coffee

Scrape the carrots and turnips. Cut the carrots in small pieces; skin the courgettes and cut them into small pieces. Cut the leeks into strips, and skin the turnips. Brown the vegetables in oil, with the mutton and chicken, add 5¼ pints (6½ pints) of water. Season with salt and red pepper, add a pinch of red paprika, 30 coriander seeds and 3 sprigs of *kosbourg* (arab parsley).

Put the semolina in a special pot, a pear-shaped earthenware one with holes to allow steam to escape, and hang it over the large pan, keeping it above the level

of the liquid. Every 30 minutes, unhook
the pot, turn the semolina out on a plate
and moisten with water, in which a pinch
of saffron has been dissolved. Knead a
good lump of butter, softened in your
hands, into the semolina, and return it to
the pot. Steam altogether for 1½ hours.

Take out some of the stock and pour
it into another saucepan in which you
have put 1 lb. chick peas. Boil this gently
for 3 hours. The peas must be well
covered with the liquid. Now chop finely
1 lb. onions and fry until they are well
coloured. Sprinkle with a good handful
of powdered sugar. Salt and pepper
lightly, and add some cumin seed. Soak
1½ oz. corinth raisins in a little warm
water about 30 minutes before serving
the *couscous*.

When everything is cooked, take out
the chicken and the shoulder of mutton.
Cut into small pieces; put aside and keep
hot. Heap the semolina in the middle of
a long dish, arrange the chick peas round
it in a circle, and heap the pieces of meat
and chicken on the semolina, as well as
the fried onions and the raisins.

Serve the stock in a tureen with some
of the vegetables in it. Serve a second
tureen with stock without vegetables into
which you stir a ladleful of Arissa coffee.
This is known as *sauce forte. Couscous* is
eaten in big bowls. Each person takes a
piece of chicken, one of mutton, a ladleful of semolina, one of chick peas, some
onions, raisins and vegetables, then
moistens his portion to his own taste

with the vegetable stock from the first
tureen. The sauce should be taken
gingerly to suit individual tastes.

SPAIN

ESCABECHE

If a tourist were asked what had struck him most about Spanish cookery,
it is possible that he would answer *gazpacho, paella* or the fish or partridge
en escabeche. But it is sauces alone which interest us. Here is one which,
moreover, is one of those surviving unaltered for centuries. I have spoken
elsewhere of *bouillabaisse*, which I have dignified with the noble name of
a sauce, rather than a soup. This is even more justified in the case of
zarzuela, which hails above all from Catalonia.

I have decribed how at one time marinades and sauces were one and the
same thing. This is why I have chosen *escabeche*. In the south-west of
France, where Spanish influence is clearly seen, fish *en escabeche* is eaten,
but never partridge. You will tell me this is because partridge is rare in
Béarn and Gascony. This is true, although sportsmen who go as far as
Sologne, Mont-de-Marsan or Condom are not unusual today when dis-
tance means less and less. But more simply, the difference is because Spain
is less conscious of the evolution of modern cookery than we are in France.
It is also true that there are plenty of partridges in Spain and that this
recipe is one of those giving more or less the same result as a marinade,
which it very closely resembles.

When, in a bygone age, game was to be preserved, it would be soaked in
marinade. So that it would not go bad, this marinade would be drained
every eight days, reboiled and cooled; then lengthened and used once
more as an immersion for the game. Sometimes it would be added at boiling point to the game, so partly cooking it.

Escabeche is nothing more or less than an application of this technique.
For this dish the partridges are quickly browned in oil, drained, put on a

dish and kept warm in the oven. There must be plenty of oil to do this properly. Continue to heat the oil until it smokes. (I would personally advise against this high temperature, but it is the foundation of the traditional recipe). Now add to the smoking oil 5 cloves of garlic, some chopped onion and a carrot sliced into very thin rounds to each bird. Fry for a moment. This means real deep frying and not the gentle colouring or browning which French cooks do by inclination. Moisten, as soon as the vegetables have taken enough colour, with a mixture of half vinegar and half water. Boil for 15 minutes with sprigs of thyme, bay leaves, parsley, pimento and salt.

Place the partridges in a terrine or a deep dish. Pour the boiling sauce over the birds, cook in a moderate oven, and then soak in the sauce for 24 hours at least. Serve cold.

The fish *escabeche* is made from sardines, mullet or mackerel. To my mind it is a second class fish dish, except when using mullet, although these are not improved by this treatment.

The fish are cleaned, dusted with flour and lightly fried. The rest of the method is exactly the same as for the partridge recipe.

SWEDEN

CRANBERRY SAUCE

My beard is Scandinavian. I happened to be in Corsica, playing at being a sea-dog, a part for which a beard is an essential ornament, when I signed a contract with the Grand Hotel in Stockholm. Since the time of Bernadotte, the chefs at the Swedish court have been depicted with beards. The last of them, whom I know very well, shaved himself on his retirement, rather as a matador cuts off his pigtail.

So, bearded I was, and bearded I had to remain for the length of my contract. But events overtook me, as meantime I made my first appearance on television. My Scandinavian contract was for three weeks; it lasted three years. My television one was for six months and lasted twelve years. So thanks to Bernadotte, I was dedicated to my beard.

But let us return to the cookery of the country. One day I nearly had a heart attack when I saw duck served with chocolate sauce. I knew this as a form of Inca cookery, but to find it at sixty degrees north called for some explanation. At that time the Grand Hotel was managed by Paul Meyer and it was to him that I addressed myself. He was a great restaurateur, one of the nineteenth-century Germans who had succeeded Urbain Dubois.

The creation of this dish was due to an accident. Among the sweets in the restaurant stood side by side the chocolate sauce intended for little *profiteroles* and the dark sauce meant for a distant cousin of Donald. The duck, having been duly carved by the expert knife of the maitre d'hôtel, was covered with chocolate sauce; the duck sauce was poured over the sweet *profiteroles*. To tell the truth, the *profiteroles* were refused! The duck was judged an inspiration. The happy diners swore that each year on the same day at the same table they would enjoy again the dish a young kitchen-hand had transformed by a comedy of errors.

I attended in a state of terror the seventh anniversary of this memorable day. I was uneasy, believe me, as to the results to be expected from participation in this exercise in local gastronomy. This was defended, and very well, too, by my very good friend Tore Wretman, who gladly produces dishes prepared in French style when he is given the opportunity; and indeed all went well.

Scandinavia is the country of *smørgasbørd*, salmon, ptarmigan, reindeer and miniature lobsters, all of them good. Swedes hold the Feast of Crayfish on August 8, when it is the done thing to cook them highly seasoned with fennel, and to eat many of them. But the recipe for cranberry sauce? Here it is. Stew the cranberries in water. Drain and strain them. Add a little sugar, a little of the juice in which they have been cooking, and then you have the traditional sauce of the country with the most beautiful girls in the world.

VIETNAM

NUOC-MAM

In discussing *Nuoc-mam*, its affinities with the Roman *garum* spring to mind. I have discussed this elsewhere in this book. It is curious to consider that *garum* completely disappeared in a few years, and no moves have been made to popularize it again. Where did it come from? Was it perhaps one of the chance finds of Alexander the Great on the banks of the Indus? I think that, more simply, the two recipes have similarities, both in the method of preparation and in the ingredients used.

A certain confusion exists to puzzle the Western gastronome. *Nuoc-mam* as known in its Far Eastern aspect was assumed to be a blending of Chinese, Indo-Chinese and Japanese cookery. But the Vietnamese say that *Nuoc-mam* is purely Indo-Chinese. The Chinese and the Japanese ignore it. Here again confusion often reigns, perhaps because the use of chop-sticks is common to these countries. *Nuoc-mam* sauce is strictly Vietnamese. There is also some confusion about soya sauce which is used more or less in quantity in all three gastronomies. The Japanese make a dish of eels not unlike that prepared with snakes in China, in which the eel, boned and split open, is kept flat by inserting small, shaped pieces of wood. It is then grilled, painted with soya sauce and put under the grill once more. The delicacy of the fish marries ill with this preparation, as in effect one eats soya with a neutral background, which is a pity.

We will now consider the resemblance between *garum* and *Nuoc-mam*. *Nuoc-mam* may be served in little flasks for pouring over soups and dishes. Often it is used in the preparation of a dish as a condiment, but mostly it is served alone in tiny cups in which food may be soaked. Used like this, *Nuoc-mam* is mixed with lime or lemon juice. It is a simple sauce, and with quite a lot of body. Perhaps we should discuss what is *garum* and what is *Nuoc-mam*. To make *garum* the entrails of flat *scomberoid* fish, of which mackerel and bonita were the most popular in the Mediterranean, were used. In the east they do not use *scomberoid* entrails, but small whole fish treated in very nearly the same way.

This process produces a juice which appears not to contain bacteria. *Nuoc-mam* is lengthened with lemon and is the traditional accompaniment of *nems*, those Indo-Chinese rolled and stuffed pancakes or chupattis. In Europe, they are called *pâtés* or *rouleaux*, or *pâtés* or *rouleaux de printemps*.

NEMS
6 servings:

10 oz. minced pork
⅓ oz. black mushrooms
1½ oz. Chinese vermicelli
6 oz. fresh shrimps
6 oz. crabmeat
1 grated carrot
1 chopped onion
2 egg yolks
pinch of glutamate
rice pancakes

Soak the mushrooms for 15 minutes and slice finely; soak the vermicelli for 15 minutes and cut it up. Boil the shrimps and shell them.

Mix all the ingredients thoroughly in a bowl. Cut up the rice cakes and soak them on a flat plate with cold water, or squeeze in a damp cloth and leave for 3 minutes in this. Allow 1 tablespoonful stuffing to each pancake; fold and roll. Fry in boiling fat for 10–15 minutes; not too many should be fried at a time. Keep warm on absorbent paper.

Alternatively for the true Indo-Chinese *nem* the more important method is to sauté the meat and the shrimps for 5 minutes before adding to the stuffing. Then roll up in an unbroken pancake and make a roll about the size of an *andouillette* or little sausage. Fry for 15 minutes and cut in four with a pair of scissors just before serving.

These rolls or stuffed pancakes are a national dish and are always served with *Nuoc-mam* prepared with the addition of a pinch of sugar, 1 chopped clove of garlic and the juice of a lemon.

Have ready a lettuce salad, well washed and dried but without any seasoning and coriander and mint leaves.

The rolls should be served very hot. To eat, hold a lettuce leaf in your left hand, then on top, according to individual taste, a coriander and mint leaf. Pick up a roll in your right hand with your chopsticks, dip it in the *nuoc-mam*, then place it on the leaves, parcel it up and eat it in your fingers.

CONCLUSION

The reader will by now have gathered from the pages of this book, that a desire for perfection, as well as technique, are inextricably bound up with the successful making of sauces.

Sauces used formerly to be elaborated at different stages in their preparation. Foundation sauces were often reduced and operations started again several times. My father simplified his techniques by reducing them to a single operation *le dépouillement*, or skimming. The reason for this is not simplification, as might be supposed, but purification. A sauce is most commonly an emulsion, to a more or less degree. If the delicate balance of an emulsion can be maintained, this will largely reduce the difficulties and the work necessary. If, on the other hand a considerable quantity of fatty substances and scum are sacrificed, not only will the volume of the sauce be reduced, but perhaps the best parts will have been thrown away.

In an age which takes slimming seriously, when you can take a holiday at a Health Farm and starve at great expense, when quacks will help you to join your ancestors for the sake of those few pounds which you alone think are superfluous, sauces have managed to survive.

When it is said that a good sauce will make a bad fish, this does not mean that the fish is positively stinking but that an insipid and ordinary fish can be transformed by a sauce into a noble dish. A good sauce can make even the gurnard or the dull tasteless *hotu* passably interesting.

There must be profound motives for the ability of sauces to survive in spite of attacks from the medical profession. I have talked about food with one of the most eminent physiologists of our time. When I asked him about sauces he said he would prefer his patients to eat a good sauce than a badly cooked grill. We know from experience that to eat an appetizing and tempting dish never did anyone harm, at any rate, not serious damage. The results, however, may be another story.

I have always thought that sauces were paleolithic in origin. They were certainly invented before fire was discovered. Was not their part precisely to make extremely simple dishes more appetizing. What was probably the very first sauce. It might well have been *garum*. Neither utensils or fire is necessary in its preparation. Leaves, flat stones, hollowed branches or logs for storage is all that is required. What leads me to believe in this theory? Am I making false assumptions? In at least two very old civilizations this sauce is found. These civilizations have no apparent link and in both cases there is no known actual recipe. *Garum* in Mediterranean countries and *nvoc-mam* in the Far East come from the same stock. It would appear that the recipe was so well-known that it was not considered worth taking the trouble to write it down.

As always it is the first step that is the most important one and it is certain that *garum*, which I take as an example of primitive sauces, evolved step by step towards the *anchoïde* of Provence and to shrimp butter. It requires little craft to serve caviar, but much talent to produce a sturgeon pâté.

To sum up, I am convinced that the sauce is the most important part of all cookery, that in fact I should be inclined to go so far as to say that it is cookery itself.

GLOSSARY

Ballottine A kind of galantine of meat, poultry, game or fish served either hot or cold. It should be boned, stuffed and rolled. When it is to be served as a cold dish, it can be glazed with aspic, sauce or jelly and garnished. The precise definition should apply only to butcher's meat, but it covers a wide range of dishes as is shown.

Beurre blanc A butter sauce from the Loire valley, originally a sauce for pike. Shallots reduced and softened are mixed with wine vinegar whisked with pale fresh farm butter.

Beurre manié Not a butter sauce but a thickening, used when a sauce is only to be thickened slightly. A piece of butter about the size of a walnut is rolled and pressed gently in flour. It is then added to the sauce shortly before serving, allowing just enough time for the sauce to simmer and the ball disappear and blend into the sauce.

Beurre noir A fish sauce, especially linked with skate. Fresh butter is heated till it turns brown and then blended with vinegar. It is also delicious with brains.

Bisque Once a general term for purées, *bisque* has come to mean particularly fish purées, served hot and lengthened into soup. It is now mostly used for shell-fish soups; *bisque d'homard, bisque d'écrevisse*, lobster and shrimp soups are perhaps the most common.

Blanc To cook *à blanc* means cooking certain meats, mainly light coloured ones, in a *court-bouillon* of flour and water with a little vinegar. This is to keep the meat from discolouring.

Blanquette A veal or chicken stew in which the meat is cut into small cubes and stewed slowly in stock with vegetables.

Bouillon Stock or broth. The liquid of the stockpot. There are vegetable, meat, poultry and fish stocks. It was also the French name for little restaurants serving meals at fixed prices and a small selection of dishes *à la carte*.

Bouilli This is an abbreviation of *boeuf bouilli*, boiled beef. The liquid in which the meat has been boiled is the bouillon.

Brochette A skewer. *En brochette* is a dish cooked and sometimes served on skewers.

Brunoise Very much the same as *mirepoix*, it is a method of preparing vegetables, such as carrots, onions, leeks and celery which are then gently fried in butter and used as a base for sauces, ragoûts and so on. The main difference is that instead of being chopped or diced they should be very finely shredded.

Capitolade A ragoût or stew made from cooked meat or poultry cut up and reheated in a sauce.

Casserole In French cookery a casserole is not only an oval or a round earthenware dish with a close-fitting lid used for braising and stewing fish, game, meat or poultry in the oven, but also, by a natural association of ideas, the name given to the food cooked in that dish as, for example, chicken casserole. There are various types of casserole of this kind, some with handles and some without.

    Casserole is also and just as commonly the name of any saucepan with straight sides and a long handle.

Cassoulet A bean stew with pork and mutton from Languedoc. The beans are the dried white ones known in England as haricot beans. There are various elaborations – game birds, ham, truffles, sausages, goose fat and vegetables, some regional, some personal, which can make *cassoulet* either a very rich or a very simple dish. The word has also come to mean the earthenware covered dish in which the food is cooked, in the oven or on the stove.

Chinois A conical sieve with a fine mesh, much used for the straining of sauces. It was originally always made of metal, but heat-proof plastic ones are now available.

Civet A ragoût which is particularly associated with game animals, hare and rabbit, although there are *civets* of game birds in some districts and even a *civet de langouste* in Languedoc. It is usually marinated in red wine and oil, and the blood of the animal is always incorporated. Jugged hare is the English equivalent.

Cocotte Round ovenproof or fireproof dishes with straight sides in which eggs, game, meat, poultry or fish are cooked and served. They are made in earthenware, porcelain, metal, steel, glass, aluminium, often with fluted sides like a soufflé dish. The small ones often have handles, and are used for individual dishes. The large ones always have lids, and the handles are more often small like ears.

Compôte Fresh or dried fruit, stewed in syrup and flavoured with vanilla, lemon or orange, cinnamon or cloves. Usually *compôtes* are served ice cold as a sweet, but they may be made into hot sweet sauces, or even as jam on tarts or bread.

Coquille In French cookery *coquille* has three meanings. Literally it is a shell – and, more precisely, a scallop. So it has come to mean both a scallop and its shell and fireproof dishes made in the shape of a deep scallop which can be filled with various mixtures such as *salpicons*, purées and so on.

Coulis A rather confusing term, it was once applied as a name for any and all sauces, but nowadays it has come to mean a purée or thick sauce, and is very often applied to fresh tomatoes reduced and strained or rubbed through a sieve.

Duxelles A mixture of shallots, parsley, onions and mushrooms, cooked slowly together in a little oil until all liquid has evaporated. It is then cooled and if absolutely dry can be stored as a standby and used for seasoning. It is also the name of a sauce made with this concentrate added to white wine and onions. It is supposed to be named after the Marquis d'Uxelles, whose cook was said to be its creator.

Fricandeau Topside of veal. It also means a dish made from loin of veal (*noix de veau*), or braised tunny (tuna) fish or sturgeon. In Belgian cookery it is also the name of a sort of meat soufflé or loaf, made from minced veal, pork, eggs and stock, baked, steamed or braised and eaten hot or cold as an entrée.

Gratin The term *gratin* means the brown coat or skin on certain dishes, which forms when they are browned in the oven or under the grill. *Au gratin* means that this method has been applied to the dish in question.

Julienne There are two meanings to this word:
(1) A clear vegetable soup made from consommé, which is garnished with finely-shredded vegetables, fried very slowly in butter.
(2) Any foodstuffs finely shredded. In the preparation of sauces it usually means a mixture of vegetables shredded and then cooked and serving as a base for stocks, *fumets* and sauces.

Marc The residue of grapes left after pressing. *Tome au raisin* is a cheese coated with the dried husks of grape pips. *Marc* is also an abbreviation of *marc eau de vie,* a liqueur distilled from the husks of grapes or the pulp of apples.

Marmite A stockpot or stewpot, usually straight-sided and with a lid. A large one, holding up to ten pints, is extremely useful and can be used for cooking chickens, as well as making stocks. Little ones for serving individual helpings of soup are called *petites marmites.* Stock pots are best made of some heavy enamelled metal, but they can also be made from earthenware as are the nicest small ones.

Mirepoix A mixture of vegetables, mostly carrots, onions, shallots, leeks and celery, chopped or diced very small, serving as a bed on which are set meat, fish or poultry to be braised or stewed. Also sautéed in butter a *mirepoix* is the base of many sauces, stocks and broths.

Miroton A stew made from cooked meats and onions. In the past this could also mean fruit dishes prepared from previously cooked fruits.

Mouli A most useful hand mill for sieving vegetables, fruit, soups or sauces. It has the advantage over an electric blender that bones, skin, fruit stones etc. are left behind and not ground into the preparation.

Nage A herb flavoured court-bouillon in which shell fish are cooked, (notably lobsters and crayfish) is called a *nage.*

Nantua, (à la) This is the generic name of dishes garnished with crayfish tails, or dressed in crayfish sauce.

Pocheuse A freshwater fish stew, cooked in wine and thickened with butter. Eel is essential and indeed should be the predominant ingredient. It is more common in districts of France near the great rivers, as the Loire valley, upper Burgundy and Bresse.

Salmis A dish often prepared, or at least finished, at the table. It is usually applied to game, and game birds in particular. They should be partly cooked, usually roasted and then finished with their own special sauce and served on croûtons of bread and garnished.

Salpicon A preparation of one or more ingredients cut up in dice and mixed and served in a blended sauce. It is often served in a case of pastry, bread or *timbales*. Also a *salpicon* can be used to stuff eggs, poultry, vegetables. The ingredients can be vegetables, fish, shellfish, meat, game, mushrooms, truffles, almost anything. They may be served hot or cold, as hors d'oeuvre or entrées.

Saupiquet This word is known as far back as the fifteenth century when it was a sauce, pure and simple, for roast rabbit and water fowl. A wine sauce was thickened with toast and seasoned heavily with spices, ginger and cinnamon. Today it is the name for a sauce for roast hare, a speciality of the south-west regions of France.

Sautoir, sauteuse A straight-sided pan, halfway between a saucepan and a frying pan, with or without a lid. It should be reasonably heavy. A most useful utensil for sautéing vegetables, meat, fish, anything in fact which needs gentle frying and simmering.

Spatula, for reduction A spatula, specially used in reducing sauces. It should be made of wood and have a flat blade perfectly straight and rectangular like a spade, or it can be made more like a little shovel with raised sides.

Terrine Again, like *marmite*, this term may lead to a little confusion in French cookery books. Strictly speaking, a terrine is an earthenware cooking pot, ovenproof but not fireproof, with a lid often with a hole in it to allow steam to escape. It should be fairly deep and without a handle, but often has little ears or lugs to help lift it out of the oven. But it can also mean simply a china or earthenware bowl. Further, the name of the dish has come to mean the food cooked in it, and especially when speaking of pâtés; a pâté *en terrine* means that the pâté has been cooked and should be served in the terrine and is not made with a pastry case.

Vambre butter Vambre was well known in the eighteenth century for the delicious quality of its butter. It was fresh and unsalted.

Verjuice This is an acid juice extracted from large unripened verjus grapes and used instead of vinegar. It has been suggested that formerly the word *verjus* meant *sauce verte* and was sold on the Paris streets.

COMPARATIVE COOKERY
TERMS AND MEASURES

BRITISH MEASURES	AMERICAN MEASURES	APPROXIMATE METRIC MEASURES
	Liquid Measures	
1 teaspoon	1¼ teaspoons	6 c.c.
1 tablespoon	1¼ tablespoons	17 c.c.
1 fluid ounce	1 fluid ounce	30 c.c.
16 fluid ounces	1 pint	·480 litre
20 fluid ounces, or 1 pint	1¼ pints	·568 litre
1⅗ pints	2 pints	1 litre
1 quart or 2 pints	2½ pints	1·136 litres
1 gallon or 8 pints	10 pints	4·544 litres

British Standard Measuring Cup is equivalent to 10 fluid ounces
American Standard Measuring Cup is equivalent to 8 fluid ounces

BRITISH MEASURES	AMERICAN MEASURES	APPROXIMATE METRIC MEASURES
	Solid Measures	
1 ounce	1 ounce	30 grammes
16 ounces or 1 lb.	16 ounces or 1 lb.	500 grammes
2 lb., 3 ounces	2 lb., 3 ounces	1 kilogram

British and American Equivalent Ingredients

BRITISH	AMERICAN
Icing sugar	Confectioner's sugar
Cornflour	Cornstarch
Sultanas	White raisins
Rusk crumbs	Zwiebach
Single cream	Light cream
Double cream	Heavy cream
Bicarbonate of soda	Baking soda
Scone	Biscuit
Soft brown sugar	Brown sugar
100 per cent wholemeal flour	Graham flour
Digestive biscuits	Graham crackers
Butter or margarine	Shortening
Other vegetable fats	Soft shortening
1 oz. cooking chocolate	1 square chocolate
$\frac{2}{3}$ oz. bakers yeast, or	
3 level teaspoonfuls dried yeast	1 cake yeast
Okra	Gumbo
$\frac{1}{3}$ oz. powdered gelatine, or level tablespoonful	1 envelope gelatine
Caster sugar	Granulated sugar
Biscuit	Cookie or Cracker
Minced meat	Ground meat
Aubergine	Eggplant

Throughout this book English measurements are given first: the American equivalent follows in brackets

VINTAGE CHART

Year	Claret	Burgundy	White Burgundy	Sauterne	Loire	Rhone	Rhine	Moselle	Champagne	Port
1945	7	5	–	6	–	7	–	–	5	7
1946	1	1	–	2	–	3	–	–	–	–
1947	5	6	–	6	–	6	–	–	5	7
1948	5	5	–	5	–	4	–	–	–	7
1949	6	5	–	6	–	7	–	–	5	–
1950	5	3	–	6	–	5	–	–	–	6
1951	0	1	–	2	–	2	–	–	–	–
1952	6	5	4	5	–	6	–	–	6	–
1953	6	4	3	5	–	6	7	6	6	–
1954	4	3	1	2	–	3	1	1	–	6
1955	6	4	4	7	–	6	5	4	6	7
1956	0	0	0	2	–	3	1	1	–	–
1957	5	5	5	4	–	6	4	4	–	–
1958	5	3	4	5	–	4	4	4	–	6
1959	6	6	5	6	6	6	7	7	7	–
1960	4	1	1	3	2	6	2	2	–	7
1961	7	6	6	6	5	7	5	4	7	–
1962	6	5	6	6	4	6	3	3	6	–
1963	1	2	3	0	1	2	3	2	–	7
1964	6	7	7	4	6	6	6	7	7	–
1965	1	1	2	0	1	2	1	1	–	–
1966	6	6	7	5	5	6	6	6	–	7
1967	6	5	6	5	6	6	5	4	–	6
1968	1	1	3	0	3	2	3	2	–	–
1969	5	7	7	6	7	5	5	5	–	–

0 = no good   7 = the best

FRESH FOOD
IN ITS BEST SEASON

	JANUARY	FEBRUARY	MARCH	APRIL	MAY	JUNE	JULY	AUGUST	SEPTEMBER	OCTOBER	NOVEMBER	DECEMBER
MEAT												
Beef	x	x	x	x	x	x	x	x	x	x	x	x
Veal		x	x	x	x	x						
Spring lamb					x	x	x	x	x			
Fed lamb	x	x	x	x						x	x	x
Pork	x	x	x	x	x	x				x	x	x
POULTRY												
Chicken	x	x	x	x	x	x	x	x	x	x	x	x
Duck	x	x	x	x	x	x	x	x	x	x	x	x
Turkey	x	x	x	x	x	x	x	x	x	x	x	x
FISH												
Bass	x	x	x	x	x	x	x	x	x	x	x	x
Carp	x	x	x	x	x	x	x	x	x	x	x	x
Cod	x	x	x	x	x	x	x	x	x	x	x	x
Dab	x	x	x	x	x	x	x	x	x	x	x	x
Eel	x	x	x	x	x	x	x	x	x	x	x	x
Flounder	x	x	x	x	x	x	x	x	x	x	x	x
(Grey) mullet	x	x	x	x	x	x	x	x	x	x	x	x
Haddock	x	x	x	x	x	x	x	x	x	x	x	x
Hake	x	x	x	x	x	x	x	x	x	x	x	x
Halibut	x	x	x	x	x	x	x	x	x	x	x	x
Herring	x	x	x	x	x	x	x	x	x	x	x	x
Lemon-sole	x	x	x	x	x	x	x	x	x	x	x	x

	JANUARY	FEBRUARY	MARCH	APRIL	MAY	JUNE	JULY	AUGUST	SEPTEMBER	OCTOBER	NOVEMBER	DECEMBER
FISH (*continued*)												
Mackerel				x	x	x	x	x	x	x	x	x
Pilchard	x	x	x	x	x	x	x	x	x	x	x	x
Salmon	x	x	x	x	x	x	x	x	x	x	x	x
Sardine				x	x	x	x	x	x	x	x	x
Sole	x	x	x	x	x	x	x	x	x	x	x	x
Trout	x	x	x	x	x	x	x	x	x	x	x	x
Whiting				x	x	x	x	x	x	x	x	
CRUSTACEANS												
Crab	x	x	x	x	x	x	x	x	x	x	x	x
Lobster	x	x	x	x	x	x	x	x	x	x	x	x
Prawns-Shrimps	x	x	x	x	x	x	x	x	x	x	x	x
MOLLUSCS												
Mussel	x	x	x	x	x	x	x	x	x	x	x	x
Oyster	x	x	x	x					x	x	x	x
Scallop	x	x	x	x	x	x	x	x	x	x	x	x
Clam	x	x	x	x	x	x	x	x	x	x	x	x
FRUIT AND VEGETABLES												
Anise	x									x	x	x
Apple									x	x	x	
Apricot						x	x					
Artichoke	x	x	x	x	x						x	x
Asparagus				x	x	x						
Avocado	x	x	x	x	x	x	x	x	x	x	x	x
Bean, Lima							x	x	x	x		
Bean, green			x	x	x	x	x	x				
Beet					x	x	x	x	x	x		
Blackberry						x						
Dewberry						x						
Loganberry						x						
Blueberry						x	x	x				

FRUIT AND VEGETABLES (continued)

	January	February	March	April	May	June	July	August	September	October	November	December
Huckleberry						x	x	x				
Broccoli	x	x	x							x	x	x
Brussels sprouts	x									x	x	x
Cabbage	x	x	x	x	x					x	x	x
Cantaloupe						x	x	x	x			
Carrot (home-grown)								x	x	x	x	
Cauliflower (home-grown)									x	x	x	x
Celery	x	x	x	x	x						x	x
Cherry					x	x	x					
Collard	x	x	x								x	x
Corn						x	x	x				
Cranberry										x	x	x
Cucumber					x	x	x	x				
Currant							x					
Eggplant						x	x	x	x			
Endive and Escarole								x	x	x		
Grapefruit (imported)	x	x	x	x						x	x	x
Grapes (home-grown)								x	x	x		
Kale					x	x				x	x	
Lettuce					x	x	x					
Melon (Cantaloupe)						x	x	x	x			
Mushroom	x	x	x	x						x	x	x
Mustard greens	x	x	x									
Okra							x	x	x	x		
Onion, dry	x	x	x							x	x	x
Onion, green					x	x	x	x				
Orange	x	x	x	x	x							

	JANUARY	FEBRUARY	MARCH	APRIL	MAY	JUNE	JULY	AUGUST	SEPTEMBER	OCTOBER	NOVEMBER	DECEMBER
FRUIT AND VEGETABLES (*continued*)												
Parsley	x	x	x	x	x	x	x	x	x	x	x	x
Parsnip	x	x	x							x	x	x
Peach						x	x	x	x			
Pear									x	x	x	x
Pea, green				x	x	x	x					
Pepper						x	x	x	x			
Persian								x	x	x		
Plum						x	x	x	x			
Potato	x	x	x	x	x	x	x	x	x	x	x	x
Sweet potato	x								x	x	x	x
Pumpkin										x		
Radish			x	x	x	x	x					
Raspberry						x	x	x				
Rhubarb			x	x	x	x						
Shallot	x	x	x	x								x
Spinach			x	x	x	x						
Squash									x	x	x	x
Strawberry			x	x	x	x						
Tangerine	x										x	x
Tomato						x	x	x	x	x		
Turnip and Rutabaga	x	x	x							x	x	x
Vatermelon						x	x	x				

INDEX

lier, 29–30
liquids:
  boiling points, 28
  choice, 13, 14
  method of adding, 13, 30
lobster: eggs, 99
lobster butter, 99
lobster sauces, 99
  recipe using, 103–6
Lyonnaise, sauce, 54

mackerel: *aïoli* with, 101
Madeira: use in sauces, 121
Madère, sauce, 55
  blending, 30
maître de chai, sauce, 96
Maltaise, sauce, 84–5, 93
marc, 122, 173
marchand de vin, sauce, 96
marinade, 18, 39
marmite, 173
Massialot:
  Le Nouveau Cuisinier Royal et Bourgeois, 44
  recipes from, 45, 88
mayonnaise, 10, 12, 99, 138
  au gratin, 135
    recipe illustrating use of, 135
  garnishes, 132
  ingredients, 86–7

  unexpected extras, 87
  preparation by blender, 86, 131
    by hand, 85
    rescue operations, 132
    using, 87–8
measures, comparative, 176–7
meat, roast:
  juices from, 110–11
  recipe illustrating use of, 112–13
Ménagier de Paris, Le : recipe from, 88
method of preparation: general, 13–14
Mexico: sauces, 155–8
Meyer, Paul, 163
Middle Ages, 19
mijoter, 30
mint sauce, 11, 146–7
mirepoix, 173
miroton, 12, 173
moelle, sauce, 126
mole, 155, 156–8
morilles, sauce, 76
  chicken in, 114
Mornay, sauce, 62
  keeping hot, 22
  lengthening, 26
  recipe illustrating use of, 61
  thickening, 31
monter, 30

The International Wine and Food Society

The International Wine and Food Society was founded in 1933 by André L. Simon, C.B.E., as a world-wide non-profit making society.

The first of its various aims has been to bring together and serve all who believe that a right understanding of wine and food is an essential part of personal contentment and health; and that an intelligent approach to the pleasures and problems of the table offers far greater rewards than the mere satisfaction of appetite.

For information about the Society,
apply to the Secretary,
Marble Arch House,
44 Edgware Road,
London, W.2